Warrior to

Patriot Citizen

by

Donna Hoffmeyer
and
Kevin Cullis

Transition your military service and skills
into your new civilian adventure!

D1310811

Title: Warrior to Patriot Civilian
Subtitle: Transition Your Military Service and Skills into Your New Civilian Adventure!

160914

ISBN-13:   978-1-5452577-39
ISBN-10:   1-5452577-36
http:// www.warriortopatriotcitizen.com

Dedication

This book is dedicated to you, the service member preparing for your future; the service member transitioning; the veteran. This is for all the jobs you have done, not because you always wanted to, but because they *had* to be done, as failure was never an option. For the missions and the deployments that resulted in many momentous events missed, but you gave it 110% anyway. This is for putting your dreams aside for another year to accomplish the mission. This is all for you.

Acknowledgements

As the saying goes, it takes a village. We want to take a moment and acknowledge our village. Without each and every one of you, this book would never have come to fruition.

Donna: Brian, thank you from the bottom of my heart for your support, endless encouragement, tired ears (I know I've worn them out many times.) and honest input. You have always been my rock.

Brady and Bianca, Mommy thanks you so much for sharing me with my computer. Brady, the day you came to me and said you wanted to write a book like me was one of my most humbling and proudest moments.

Mom and Dad, thank you for teaching me to never give up.

To all my awesome friends, especially Jen Chenevert, Kathy Jimenez, Patricia Cashion, Terry Winnett, and "Oz." Thank you for being my cheerleaders and giving brutal honest opinions when it was needed.

To Kevin, my coauthor, whose enthusiasm gave birth to this project and added momentum to it throughout this project.

Kevin: To Ruth, who has been by my side, "keeping egg in my stomach and not on my face," through 33 years of marriage, and the many and various twists and turns of our transitions since leaving the service.

To my Dad. I came to realize, after he was gone, that I really am a "chip off the old block" when it comes to my creative writing.

But mostly, to Donna, my coauthor. Her veteran and service member surveys brought in a depth that my "fog of war" of ideas and words could not be clearly seen until we neared completion. It was only looking back that I realized her efforts has been our backbone. For that, I am grateful and she has my deepest admiration and respect.

Both: To our editor, Floyd Largent, thank you for your skills and patience. Your positive words and insight kept us moving forward.

Our guest writer, Judy Hansen, thank you for your expertise in the world of psychology.

To Sheila Stephens and the Valkyrie Initiative, thank you for letting us be part of something bigger than all of us. We hope this book provides guidance and resources to the many warrior the Valkyrie Initiative will serve in the future.

And finally, but by far not least, a big shout out goes to Mitch Durfee, Raymond Viel, and all the Service Members and Veterans who took the time to share their experiences and give advice to others. This book would not be possible without you.

Table of Contents

Foreword .... **xi**

1. Introduction **1**

George Washington: General and Citizen 2
U.S. Military Service.. 8
Your Action Plan 10

2. First Transition: Civilian to Warrior **11**

Basic or Officer Training... 12
Military Career Training.. 16
First Term or Career Service 19

3. Second Transition: Warrior to Civilian **21**

Decision Time: Prepare for DABDA 22
Denial, Anger, Bargaining, Depression, Acceptance 23
Mindset: How to Transition from Military
to Civilian Life. 27
Getting Organized 31
Know Who and Where You Are 31
Know Where You're Going 52
Action Plan 60

4. You're Hurt/Wounded; Now What? **63**

The Importance of Connecting 70
Action Plan 72

5. Your Health: Physical, Mental, and Financial .. **75**

Exercise 76
Eat Healthy 78

Think Healthy 82
Sleep Healthy 84
Mental Health 87
Financial Health 93
Action Plan 97

6. Doing What You Love 101

Growth versus fixed mindset 103
Talents first, passions second 105
Civilian to military, military to civilian 111
Preparing for your new civilian career 112
Civilian cultures differ from military culture 112
From "Quiet Professional" to Selling Yourself 114
Assessing military talents, skills, and life experiences 116
    Keep and Honor 116
    Keep and Translate 117
    Drop or Change 118
    Depreciate and Lessen 120
    Ignore or Bury 121
Action Plan 123

7. Connect with your Community 127

Connect with individuals 128
Connect with organizations 135
Connect with your grassroots community 137
Action Plan: 139

8. "Charlie Mike" in the Marketplace 143

Moving from military to civilian 144
Find a job, work, a new career, and an adventure 145
Start your own business as an entrepreneur 146
The Business Model Generation (BMG) is for startups 150
Business Planning (BP) is for businesses and investors 153
25+ Businesses you can start for under $1,000 155

Failure: When/where it is/is not an option? 157
Action Plan: 159

9. Your adventure in the marketplace 163

Marketing Yourself 163
Social media platforms 164
    LinkedIn. 165
    Facebook 167
    Your own web site 167
    Other social media sites 168
Social media networking 169
Moving forward with your new adventure 171
Action Plan: 173

10. Success Story - Warrior to Patriot Citizen ... 177

    Veteran Success Story - Grunts Move Junk 177

11. Veteran's quips, advice, and letters 193

Reasons for leaving 193
Preparing for transition 197
Continue to focus on learning and education 204
Best and worst advice 205
Easiest and hardest part of transition 209
Good advice 212

12. Resources 223

What's Next? 223
Organizations and Web Sites to Help 223
Educational resources 224
Employment 224
Entrepreneurship and startups 227
Health 229
Women's veterans groups 231
General resources 232

Web sites 232
Multi-service resources.. 234
Services 234
Studies.. 236
Transition resources 236
Volunteer/Nonprofit 237

Appendix. Our National Startup & Veteran Legislation 243

1700s: Startup Nation and Revolution........................... 246
1800s Wars, Conflicts, and Legislation 250
1900s Wars, Conflicts, and Legislation 257
2000s Wars, Conflicts, and Legislation 266

Foreword

I was medically retired as a Special Agent with the Bureau of Alcohol, Tobacco, Firearms and Explosives (ATF) due to injury on the job. The transition was traumatic. Suddenly, others were in control of the most important decisions of my life, and there followed endless days in hospitals, doctors' offices, and rehab facilities. This was not the worst part, however.

Because of this injury, I was no longer able to do the job I loved, the job I performed better than anything I'd ever done, and the one which afforded me access to my buddies, those with whom I had bonded, those who I knew always had my back... relationships I had found nowhere else. "What will I do now?" I asked. More than that, "Who will I be now?" Law enforcement is a profession that goes beyond a job. For most, it is an identity. The law enforcement officer has, in most states, peace officer status. This means he or she is required to be armed even when not on duty, and to respond to a felony in progress when within view. This means we never remove our badge, even when not wearing one. Being an officer, or in my case, a Special Agent, becomes who we are. Therefore, when we are no longer able to work in our field, no longer have the vehicle to exercise the identity created by that profession, an identity ideal for our warrior personality and skills, we can struggle with many issues.

As I healed, I met agents and military personnel in the same situation, enduring the same struggles. I began The Valkyrie Initiative with the goal of addressing this struggle and alleviating it with jobs and life skills training, recreational therapy, stress relief and relaxation techniques, as well as nutritional counseling...all toward a holistic approach to wellness and optimal performance gains, and to show the world and the veteran and first responder that they are not broken forever. We also work with families. As I spoke with more and more of these men and women, I realized that their stories need to be told.

When I began The Valkyrie Initiative's book series, American Warrior Journal, I envisioned three books of personal stories. The first by veterans, called *Still Standing*; the second by first responders; and the third by family members. I wanted to show the public the world of this unique group of men and women… their experiences and challenges, their no-quit attitude, the strength of their mindset and "warrior" personality, and the resiliency with which they rise from the trauma and injuries many have faced.

More than that, my goal was to show other veterans and first responders hope for a successful transition from military or police/fire/EMT experience to civilian life. I wanted to show them they are still who they were while in service to their country; they merely need to find the place where their special mindset, skills and tremendous work ethic, dedication, and desire for challenge, for a mission, "fits" in the civilian world. I envisioned a series to showcase a large number of warriors' stories and reveal how they are "still standing" through it all.

When I learned of Donna and Kevin's book project, *Warrior to Patriot Civilian*, I realized that this could be the fourth book in our series. After reading their material, I decided it should be the first. While other books for transition exist, most concentrate on writing resumes and dressing for interviews and other necessary tools for job hunting. This book is different. It is written at a deeper level of transition: one that addresses the veteran him- or herself, and how specific skills may be used during transition. The topics covered-range from types of skill sets acquired in former military positions that can be transferred to civilian jobs and careers all the way to stages of grief that may be experienced in this transition. It is an important concept to grasp—their feelings are normal—and the authors reveal means of navigating them, something that definitely separates this book from others.

Another unique difference is that mental mindset is addressed in personal interviews included by those who have made successful transitions. This may be one of the more unique parts of this book, the experiences shared by others. Donna and Kevin have compiled stories that are interesting and enlightening, as is the best practice information for planning and moving forward.

Perhaps the best parts of this book (I emphasize perhaps, because there are so many "bests") include multiple resources located around the nation and its inclusion of Action Plans. In these plans, the authors cover mental, physical and financial wellbeing, addressing the health of the warrior as a whole, and providing steps to achieve it.

This book fulfills my goal of showing the world the strength of the warfighter by providing many interviews with those who have transitioned and a few currently going through the process. It fulfills my goal of revealing the strength and resiliency inherent in this unique personality, outlining the process as it has been experienced by others.

Additionally, it stretches beyond all of this by providing information and resources for making transition a successful reality. It shows the veteran how it is possible to remain the same person who protected our nation while capitalizing on the possibility for growth and change arising from his or her experience. Identity has not changed, merely location of service. The warrior identity remains, and transition of those skills used in service to the homeland to which the warfighter has previously sworn allegiance, is transferred to living their dreams within a civilian framework, however that may look to the individual. With the information contained in this book, and a little help from friends and family, this is entirely possible. This knowledge is most important for identity retention, something with which many veterans struggle upon leaving their military roles and lifestyle.

This book is a must-read for anyone transitioning from military to civilian life… whether you are retiring, medically retiring/separating, or deciding to separate. The research, resources, and tools contained in its pages will guide you as you find your passion and begin your new mission…your next adventure!

I know you will enjoy it as much as I did. Look for the upcoming books in this series!

Sheila L Stephens
M.A. Criminal Justice
Ph.D. Candidate in Performance Psychology
President and CEO of The Valkyrie Initiative
http://thevalkyrieinitiave.org
Private Investigator, Security Consultant and Speaker
President/CEO of SaferSecurity, Inc.
Former police officer and ATF Special Agent
Professor of Criminal Justice
Author of *The Book of Private Investigation*, Adams Media

1. Introduction

I still remember the refrain of one of the most popular barrack ballads of that day, which proclaimed most proudly that "Old soldiers never die; they just fade away." And like the old soldier of that ballad, I now close my military career and just fade away, an old soldier who tried to do his duty as God gave him the light to see that duty. — General Douglas MacArthur

Fade away... sounds noble, doesn't it? But our country has changed a great deal since its founding. Today, modern medicine enables most of us in live a lot longer than people did in the days of Douglas MacArthur; so much so that many people in the 21st century go on to work for another 20 years or more after military service and retirement. Today, fading away doesn't pay the bills or feed the family, even with a retirement check.

If you fall into this category, or think you will, doesn't it behoove you to make sure your second career is a product of your passions and skills? Many individuals enter the service with a known set of talents and abilities, and through the course of their service career, discover or develop talents and abilities they weren't aware of previously.

Before we dive too deep, let's look back in history at one of the strongest military leaders and entrepreneurs of America's national startup era: George Washington. Yes, you read that correctly. Good ol' GW already had quite the head for business before the Revolutionary War, and his military service and experience helped him learn first-hand the logistics needed to keep improving a newborn country.

George Washington: General and Citizen

Before the Revolutionary War. George Washington never did want to:

> ...*aspire to command prosperity. He thought of the economy as a kind of self-sustaining machine. Government's job was to keep it clean, well-oiled, and secure. The people fueled it, set it in motion, and—after a tithe to the government to fund its expenses—reaped the benefits. The operation was both natural and simple. Always, though, he exhorted the people to keep one principle in mind: work together, or perish separately. Washington was the unifier to guide them.*[1]

Washington was born at his father's plantation on Pope's Creek in Westmoreland County, Virginia, on February 22, 1732.[2] Not much is known about his early childhood, other than some popular fables ("I cannot tell a lie"). When he was a young man, he applied himself to a number of trades. He became a surveyor at age 17, but showed early signs of entrepreneurship. In an effort to establish himself as a member of the landed gentry, he worked hard, saved his money, and bought unclaimed land. Later, he would serve in various military positions and gain significant experience. It is important to note that each time he served in the military, he ended up resigning his commission. How he handled each transition makes him a perfect example of how to translate the skills learned while serving to your next adventure.

Washington became a farmer/entrepreneur, and spent the years between 1759 and 1775 as a gentleman farmer at Mount Vernon. He worked constantly to both improve and expand the farm's structures and the size of the plantation. Washington was an innovative farmer,

---

[1] *First Entrepreneur* by Edward G. Lengel, p. 5
[2] mountvernon.org

switching from tobacco to wheat as his main cash crop, and was diligent in experimenting with tools, livestock breeding, crop rotation, new crops, and fertilizers in order to improve his farming operations. He also expanded the work of the plantation to include flour milling, which ground 278,000 pounds of branded flour annually. He shipped his flour throughout America and, unusually during colonial times, also exported to Europe.[3] In an effort to make Mount Vernon a more profitable estate, he successfully ventured into commercial fishing. In addition, Washington built one of the largest distilleries in America. At its peak, his distillery produced over 11,000 gallons of rye whiskey, becoming one of his most successful enterprises. At the time, he ran "the largest whiskey distillery in America."[4].

During and After the Revolutionary War. On June 14, 1775, Washington was appointed commander of the Continental Army, and wrote home to Martha that he expected to return safely to her in the fall. However, the responsibilities of command kept him away from Mount Vernon for more than eight years, battling both on the ground against the British, and on the political front with the Continental Congress over funding.

Following the end of the Revolutionary War, Washington was ready to transition back to civilian life:

On December 23, 1783, Washington strode into the statehouse at Annapolis, Maryland and surrendered his military commission to a grateful Congress. In front of the gathered congressmen, Washington declared, "Having now finished the work assigned me, I retire from the great theatre of Action—and bidding an Affectionate farewell to this

---

[3] Harlow Giles Unger, *The Unexpected George Washington: His Private Life*
[4] mountvernon.org/the-estate-gardens/distillery/

August body under whose orders I have so long acted, I here offer my Commission, and take my leave of all the employments of public life."[5]

While Washington had a keen interest in agriculture before the Revolutionary War, his military time and experience were not wasted. As with anyone who leaves their hometown and "sees the world," military service gave him a different perspective on life—based on observing what people in other locales were doing and how one could connect with and learn from them. Following years of conflict and hardship, others were also ready to embrace change. After the War, "Washington's ... rehabilitation of Mount Vernon progressed from repairing the physical improvements of his plantation to a reconsideration of his entire mode of farming. The end of the war triggered an interest amongst educated and wealthy American planters and gentleman farmers in agricultural reform."[6].

But all progress requires those who have the wherewithal (i.e., Research and Development funding) to do the research and find ways to improve the industry. Those who eked out a living as farmers were reluctant to change, because any change meant the potential loss of their current levels of production if things didn't pan out. The poorer farmers' resistance to change was realistically there, no different from today's entrepreneurs; so those with the necessary resources took on the endeavor for the benefit of all.

Even after leaving his command and returning to his estate to farm, Washington was never out of earshot of what was occurring on the political front of his new country. This isn't much different from most of today's service members, who remain connected with service to others even after leaving military service.

---

[5] mountvernon.org/revolutionarywar/10facts
[6] mountvernon.org "George Washington and Agriculture"

Washington was popular enough to be crowned a king, but he relinquished his power readily. He left Annapolis and went home to Mount Vernon with the determined intention of never again serving in public life. This one act, without precedent in modern history, made him an international hero. But Washington kept his ear to the ground, paying close attention to what was going on in the heart of the new nation. The Articles of Confederation, drafted in mid-1776 and formally ratified by all 13 states by early 1781, had created a weak union—and he saw his nation gradually disintegrate, unable to collect revenue or pay its debts. Political reforms were needed, so Washington again left private life and presided over a Constitutional Convention, taking four months to create an energized Constitution. He hoped to retire to private life afterward, but was unanimously elected as America's first President. He remains the only President in American history ever to have been elected by the unanimous voice of the people. He served two terms, from 1789-1797. His retirement from public life was sadly short-lived; he became sick during an outing in the cold weather, and on December 14, 1799, George Washington passed away. He was 67 years old.[7]

Washington: Veteran Advocate. Washington fought for what he felt was right, which included securing financial remuneration for those who served during the Revolutionary War. A hint of his affinity for service members was displayed when an anonymous letter circulated in his camp at Newburgh, N.Y. in the spring of 1783, suggested an armed protest. Washington had pleaded with Congress for months for provisions, uniforms, and back pay for those under his command. When the letter was revealed, he gathered together his officers and wrote:

---

[7] mountvernon.org. See *The Biography of George Washington.*

> *If this, then, be your treatment while the swords you wear are necessary to the defense of America, what have you to expect from peace, when your voice shall sink and your strength dissipate by division— when those very swords, the instruments and companions of your glory, shall be taken from your sides and no remaining mark of military distinction be left but your wants, infirmities and scars? Can you then consent to...grow old in poverty, wretchedness and contempt?"*[8]

Both during and after the War, the weakened American government was unable to pay the veterans, because mounting debts and conflicts arose between American republican ideals and the military institutions veterans represented. Veterans were caught in the middle of a public political debate that left them feeling abandoned by the nation they had sacrificed to create. The first veteran's pension movement began during the war, when officers lobbied Congress in 1779 for half-pay for life. Public outcry charged officers with attempting to establish a military aristocracy on the backs of the civilian population.[9] It wasn't until decades after the Constitution and the Bill of Rights in 1787 that the Federal government was able to provide some remuneration for veterans, as public sentiment changed with the Congressional passage of the 1818 Revolutionary War Pension Act, marking an important shift in American political culture.

> *Americans began to see them [veterans] as a proper and necessary way to repay the debt of gratitude the nation owed to those who had fought and suffered to create it. So strong was public support for pensions that the program even weathered a serious scandal in 1820. In the end, more than 20,000 Revolutionary War veterans received pensions.*[10]

---

[8] *What Do We Owe Our Vets?* See at historynet.com.;
[9] *The Unfinished Revolution: Revolutionary War Veteran Entitlements.* See nps.gov
[10] h-net.org; See *Images of Veterans in (Early) American Society.*

About 217,000 militia, Continental Army soldiers, and others served at the height of the War,[11] including privateers (sometimes called corsairs or buccaneers)—private people or ships authorized by government letters of marque to attack foreign vessels during wartime. Privateering was a way of mobilizing armed ships and sailors without commissioning vessels into regular service as warships.

Going forward. By now, you're probably wondering, "What does that mini-history lesson have to do with transitioning from the military to civilian life?" The answer is, a lot. Washington may have had raw entrepreneurial talent, but it was his military experience that honed his operational, organizational, critical thinking, and leadership skills to give him the tools to mold his capabilities in the market and allow him to become a more successful private citizen. The same can be said for you as you exit the military. You can take all your learned and earned skills, couple them with your passion, and strike out into a new career of your choosing.

The purpose of this book is to give you the resources to assist you in setting in motion the steps needed to determine your financial needs, identify your passion, translate your military skills into civilian terminology, and connect financial requirements, passion, and skills to find civilian employment that fulfills your monetary and personal needs. Throughout this book there will be quips, quotes and stories from veterans in all branches of service who have already worked through the transition, as well as those who are currently going through the process. Who better to learn from?

---

[11] va.gov. See *America's War* from VA Public Affairs Office PD.

U.S. Military Service

The US military service member is unique in the world, in that any service member or veteran is someone who, at one point in his/her life, wrote a blank check made payable to "The United States of America" for an amount of "up to and including my life." That's an enormous commitment all by itself. However, many civilians don't understand that this comes with a lot of "voluntolds" – assignments, deployments, duties, re-training, becoming the "expert" when staffing is short, etc. The service member has an ingrained "do what it takes to get the mission done" mentality. Very few received every assignment they asked for, every schooling or specialty training they applied for; seemingly, nearly every service member has a "voluntold" story. What many may or may not realize is it is those unplanned paths that provide the service member with a greater breadth of knowledge.

Donna: I'll use myself as an example. I am a nurse by trade. After a four-year break from AD, I came back to the Reserves. Ten months into my reserve commitments, I was asked to be Chief of Medical Readiness in my squadron. I had a bit of readiness knowledge from my aeromedical evacuation days, but all in all, I had zero 'true" readiness experience. My unit leadership were aware of it, too. But they were in a bind and needed someone ASAP, so tag, I was it. I suppose I voluntold myself on that one. Not looking back, I grabbed the regulations, a notepad, pen, and prayer, and jumped in with both feet. It was the fastest/steepest spin-up I ever experienced. It is also one of the experiences I am most grateful for having survived. It has helped me in every other job since. Furthermore, being thrown into the fire gave me the confidence to enter unknown territory and be resourceful enough to become an expert on many subjects in a short amount of time.

Kevin: Having transitioned into the civilian world, I recognized early on that the ability to adapt and overcome is a skill in demand, but civilian employers do not always assume former military personnel possess it. You hear from civilians and CXOs that military members may not be well suited to changing marketplace conditions, but this isn't necessarily true. For example, when I was working for Apple, during the introduction of the new iPhone we were given two hours to change our store's layout and two hours to learn what we could about the iPhone in order to expertly demonstrate its capability and sell it to a very eager, tech-savvy line of customers.

B.O., Senior Engineer, 36 years USA & Army National Guard CMS: While still serving, accept every opportunity to go to training and leadership schools you can. I have three MOS's, I attended every Noncommissioned Officer Course the Army offered, and attended countless other schools that gave me special skill identifiers and qualified me to compete for and earn assignments most NCOs would never experience.

The point is, breadth of knowledge can translate into skills and experience when properly applied. The more we learn, the more valuable we become. So while we may end up in jobs we originally had no intention or interest in doing, realize the skills (and confidence) developed will be invaluable in future work – both in and out of the military. They may be the very skills and knowledge needed to pursue your passion… your future mission in the civilian sector.

Your Action Plan

Donna: As we write this book, my husband and fellow military member has just submitted his retirement paperwork. Although it's exciting to see him prepare to enter a new phase of work, it raises the blood pressure a point or two. The big question arises … "Will he be able to find a job in this market?" Followed by, "Will he be able to find a job that utilizes his skills and fulfills his passion?" (Seriously, who wants to deal with a partner who isn't happy with their work?) These questions don't just miraculously get answered. It takes knowing what you want to do and having a plan to reach your goals. The key to all this is to be brutally honest with yourself. If you delivered customer service in the military, but found working with people was taxing on your soul, perhaps you have a passion for working with animals. Your goal is to translate the customer service skills you developed into civilian terminology that will assist you in achieving your mission of working with animals. On the other hand, maybe you're a Special Forces service member and quickly realized you wanted to continue operating in an adrenaline-rushed environment. The goal is still the same: translate the various skills you gained while serving into a terminology civilian employers understand.

To help you develop a road map for success, we have placed an Action Plan at the end of each chapter. You're strongly encouraged to accomplish it in sequence after covering each subject, as the subsequent chapters will build on earlier concepts. This will help you stay on track with your goals as you work toward achieving your new mission.

2. First Transition: Civilian to Warrior

The mind is not a vessel to be filled, but a fire to be kindled.—
Plutarch

Somehow, you made the decision to enter the service. Maybe it was what you'd planned all along as a child, or someone encouraged you to do it later. Perhaps your parents saw ROTC as an opportunity and signed you up unknowingly (*Donna:* Yes, this actually happened to a college friend). Possibly you had nowhere else to go with your life, and wanted to try something other than what you were currently doing—or it was a last-minute decision, a calling you simply needed to heed.

Whatever your reasons for entering the service—good, bad, or indifferent—you joined a career only a select few attempt. There are roughly 322 million Americans as of December 2015, but only about two million Active, Guard, and Reserve service members are on watch defending the nation. That's less than-one half of 1% of the population. Another 22 million or so served in the past—about 7% of the population. Couple these small numbers with advances in technology which are enabling us to decrease the size of the force, and the result is fewer and fewer individuals willing and able to make the same incredible commitment and sacrifice you did. In turn, that also means there are fewer and fewer individuals with the same character and skills you possess.

Basic or Officer Training

Deciding to serve your country is an enormous decision to make at such a young age. But what an exciting time! Once that decision was made, you became the property of the U.S. Government. Can you remember how you felt when you made the decision? Did you swell with pride when you took your oath? Were you anxious and excited when you left for basic? Or, perhaps your first experience was Plebe summer at the Academy, or ROTC Field Training. Regardless of how you entered military service, no doubt there was a mix of trepidation and excitement as you wondered about the adventures you would experience. Think back to your thoughts as you were stepping off the bus, getting your first of many verbal "instructions," and seeing an entire community of meticulously like-dressed people. Think about how you felt when you were graduating. Were you amazed at the amount of discipline, skill and confidence you developed in your brief time in uniform? What about after tech school, specialty training, or any of your other schooling that allowed you to enhance your skills? Whether you've completely enjoyed the military or just tolerated it as a means to an end, you benefitted. Every learning opportunity put more skills in your career "toolbox" —some of which you used all the time, and some intermittently—and little did you realize at the time that many of them would benefit you in your future as a civilian.

Donna: Kevin and I joined for different reasons. I was a financially poor, newly graduated nurse with college loans, who needed a job at a time the civilian sector was attempting to contain medical costs by hiring more LPNs and CNAs, and fewer RNs. Like many new graduates, I was idealistic and wanted to find the "right" first job. For me, it had to fulfill my travel-bug desires as well as allow me to gain amazing experiences and continue to get paid. Not asking too much, right? After watching my friends receive numerous "thank-you-for-applying-but-we-have-no-openings" letters, coupled with my romantic job desires, I saw my choices rapidly narrowing. I was soon down to the military or the Peace Corps. Both allowed me to fulfill my desire to travel. While the latter was very appealing to me, it lost in the end, because I had no experience as a nurse and it didn't pay. Besides, I couldn't continue to move to new jobs and still keep moving up the career ladder. The military provided all of that, plus it developed pride, confidence, and patriotism; the latter came when the military "raised me," and I truly understood what my commitment meant.

Over the last 15 years, like everyone, I have had my challenges, and I questioned whether being in the military was the right thing for me. I even took a four-year hiatus when I felt I'd stopped having "fun." It was during my time working as a civilian that I could see and truly appreciate what the military had given and brought out in me: discipline, confidence, and dedication, to name just a few things. One of my "ah ha" moments occurred when we were still short-staffed on the medical floor, even after we brought in the call nurse. My first thought was, *Call in more nurses…* simple as that. Yeah, not so much. It didn't occur to me they could refuse to come in to work. Refusing to come in is never an option in the military; if you aren't on leave, you're available. Period.

The first thing the military teaches all of us in basic or officer training is discipline and teamwork. We all have at least one story of a single person's failure being a failure for everyone. When we leave our initial training, we have a solid understanding of the importance of structure, and why each person is critical to the success of the team. The person at the top of the pyramid is only as good as the foundation supporting them.

The enlisted go on to technical school, where they learn the required skills for their trade (aircraft maintenance, medic, infantry, etc.). Officers have a couple of avenues for advancement. Some go into internships/orientation (e.g. nurses), some get on-the-job training, and others complete further schooling. This is the beginning of becoming a subject matter expert (SME). Technical skills will continue to be honed with experience.

Over the years, there is less emphasis on technical training and more on leadership training. At this point, each service member is an SME. They are now teaching others and taking on supervisory roles. Moving along the continuum, the vast majority move further away from technical skills and into greater leadership roles. Leadership training has been occurring on some level throughout their careers, and although no one is completely prepared for their first leadership role, they have been armed with basic tools to build upon.

You all know how this works. My point is, service members receive more fellowship, leadership, and teamwork training than our civilian counterparts. These key ingredients are measured and poured into us from the very beginning and continue to be mixed in throughout our careers. Only after we have the basic leadership tenants down does the military technical training get introduced. What civilian company do you know of that starts out on Day One with discipline and teamwork training, infused with leadership training, before moving on to technical training? Most companies start you out with technical/on-the-job training, before giving you "accessory" training. If anything, you most likely have to learn leadership training on your own in the civilian world, as this is a "cost center" for businesses.

So service members are ahead of the game in our specialized and followership/leadership training, and when we come out of the military, we should have an abundance of work waiting for us—right? We wish that were the case! The challenge comes when all those military skills have to be translated into viable civilian skills. If we can't communicate those skills in a manner a civilian understands, then we're of little value to a civilian company. Proper translation is important for maximum opportunity. We'll discuss this in detail later in the book.

Kevin: Donna's story isn't much different from mine. Most of my friends were heading to college after high school, but I was through with school—or so I thought. My parents suggested going into the Air Force after high school under the delayed enlistment program. As a typical teenager, I didn't have much motivation... that is, until I finished basic and went home and right away told my mother how dusty my room was. I had what I would call a "low level" form of patriotism; a stronger sense of it didn't kick in until about halfway through my enlistment. It started slowly and grew from there as I matured and learned about being a leader.

I started out as a Crew Chief on F-4Ds at Hill AFB, Utah, coming back from Thailand after the Vietnam conflict. From there, I crewed RF-4Cs at RAF Alconbury, England, and then finally landed back in the Continental United States (CONUS) at Hill AFB again; this time, I was working on F-16A/Bs. My problem? Even though I was beginning to see the small steps of leadership the USAF instills in you, I failed to see the many challenges ahead, even when working on brand new F-16s. I wanted more, so I decided to get out; and since I didn't know what I was going to do with my life, I did what I thought others would do: I started college.

At freshman college orientation, when I was told to do something, I followed the instructions—and I saw how much more responsible I had become regarding following instructions compared to the lackadaisical incoming freshmen I encountered. It was then that I realized I had acquired far more responsibilities and drive in the USAF than most of my friends from high school. This rang true when compared to those entering college, along with those I worked with at my new civilian job. It wasn't until I got out of the military that I saw

15

from the outside looking in what I learned and accomplished. I finally recognized what I was responsible for in the USAF and what it all meant. Hindsight is always 20/20. Just like living overseas, when you're away from something for a while, you understand what you have/had and appreciate it more.

This is not to say I had it all figured out when I entered college. I still had much to learn, so I entered the USAF ROTC program. This's where the initial foundation was laid for learning the upper level of knowledge of organizational structures, leadership and officer responsibilities. As a civilian, you rarely get this type of information from businesses unless you work for larger corporations that have the budget and time to get you this training. In most cases, it's sink or swim for you.

Military Career Training

Once you fulfilled your initial military training, you were assigned a military career. Out of the hundreds of career opportunities available—whether you were Army infantry, Marine tank crewman, Navy diver, Coast Guard boatswain mate, or Air Force TAC-P —you were trained in how the military runs its operations and how you were expected to perform your job.

These represent the second set of skills developed in the military— those referred to earlier as technical skills. As you are transitioning, you need to ask yourself what type of civilian work you want to pursue. If you're looking for civilian work requiring technical skills, then it will be very important to identify and translate these skills into terminology familiar to the civilian world.

A word of caution here: don't limit yourself to the actual job itself. For example, if your job in the military is aircraft maintenance, don't limit yourself to "fixing XXX aircraft." Think about the multitasking that occurs, the quick decision-making and attention to detail required.

16

Did you complete specialized training and exercise critical thinking skills to figure out what was wrong with the aircraft, vehicle, generator, etc.? Remember, you need to emphasize the SKILLS, not the job you did in the military. The job developed your skills. You can use the skills you've learned to go into a job that may be completely different from what you did in the military. The only similarity between the two maybe the skills utilized to get the mission done. The key here is to generalize your platform. Here are some examples of civilian jobs real former service members now perform in relation to their military responsibilities:

Military to Civilian Job Conversion

Military Job	Civilian Job
Army Infantry	Veteran Recruiter
Recruiter	Human Resources
Aeromedical Technician	Medical Simulator Company and Consultant
Loadmaster	Airline Cargo Handler
Nurse	Massage Therapist/Business Owner

Some careers will be direct transfers. Nurse, lawyer, doctor, pilot, lab technician, radiology technician, and firefighter are some examples of careers that can transfer directly to the civilian world. In the civilian world, your Airframe and Powerplant license (A&P) crosses over nicely. You just need to take the test. What about getting an EMT for Navy Corpsmen or USAF medics? The wide array of administrative duties are still administrative duties wherever you go, i.e. an Office Manager. The key issue for a service member is to generalize their platform (weapons loading becomes medium equipment operating or ship cargo loading, for example). Even though the technical skills may not need as much translating, it's still important to take stock of what your skills are and translate them for your new mission in life.

In some careers, you may be more advanced than your civilian counterparts. An Air Force basic medic is a perfect example. The civilian counterpart is an emergency medical technician basic (EMT-B) or certified nurse's aide (CNA). They do basic patient care (vital signs, wound care, intake/output, bed baths, etc.), basic trauma care (applying cervical collars, splints, spine boards, etc.), and a narrow scope of medications (EMTs only). However, unlike their civilian counterpart, the military medic does all that *plus* starts IVs, inserts Foley catheters, intubates, gives a larger scope of medications (commensurate to their skill level), performs uncomplicated delivery of newborns, sutures, places casts, and a host of other skills that aren't within the scope of practice for an EMT-B or CNA. Many medics may find themselves working *below* their skill-set abilities, and may feel undervalued. Therefore, it's critical to know what skill set is required for your future civilian work.

Don't just capture your skill-set, but also capture the types or functions of the items you work with, such as dealing with mechanical items or building berms or dugouts for your troops for protection. While most people may not consider building an outpost a significant skill, it would be if you were to head into nature and construct buildings for hikers on a trail.

Remember what we said earlier: leadership skills have been taught to you from the very start of your military journey. Capture those skills! Whether you self-supervised, were a Platoon Leader of 10, the Battalion Commander of hundreds of people, or the Fleet or Wing Commander of thousands, it's important to document those leadership skills. This will make you more marketable for job advancement in the civilian sector, and the more numbers you can show to an employer, the greater your chances of standing out from the pack.

A word on self-supervision: don't sell yourself short if you're in a "one-deep" position. You still acquire many of the leadership skills required to be successful. One must be self-motivated, self-directed, need limited guidance, resourceful, network savvy, and maintain the ability to research the right answers, learn quickly, and be organized. You've got plenty of leadership skills! Yes, you may never have dealt directly with supervising a group; however, if you can be successful in a one-deep shop, then the odds are in your favor that you'll have the determination to learn and be successful when placed in charge of a group.

The military trains us in followership/leadership skills. In the civilian world, there may be less leadership and more followership skills needed, depending on a company's culture. We'll get more in-depth about figuring out your skill-set later in the book.

First Term or Career Service

Whether you were a one-term service member or career military, you're still a veteran, and no one can take that—and your developed set of skills—away from you. When you leave the service, success is about continuing to grow and improve yourself to your fullest possible extent—not just for yourself, but for others, too. This is very evident in both the Israeli and the U.S. militaries. As Israeli entrepreneur Jon Medved—who sold several startups to large American companies— told us, "When it comes to U.S. military résumés, Silicon Valley is illiterate. It's a shame. What a waste of the kick-ass leadership talent coming out of Iraq and Afghanistan! The American business world doesn't quite know what to do with them."[12]

---

[12]*Startup Nation,* by Senor and Singer, p. 79.

19

Knowing and being aware of this attitude will help prepare you for your new mission in life. Some will like your military service; others may not.

Kevin: I have had some people imply that being in the military meant I had to be stupid. Some were even antagonistic, trying to prove their views in front of others. There's a far cry between being stupid and being ignorant of a subject (like physics or chemistry) that a new job you're interested in might require. Not knowing something doesn't mean you can't think and learn.

Don't let negative hiring bias get you down. Some organizations self-select against your more valuable expertise for other people of lesser caliber. They get what they pay for; lower pay can equal low-quality performance. It's better to work for someone who wants you than for someone that thinks poorly of you. The best thing you can do for yourself is to network like crazy before and after you leave the service. Being a veteran will become a badge of honor—but expect service rivalry and trash talk when you meet fellow veterans and find out when and where they served. Of primary concern is ensuring you remember that as a veteran, you're in a band of brothers and sisters representing a tiny population of today's American population.

You should not only hold your head up high as a result, but support and connect with those who were in your sister services.

3. Second Transition: Warrior to Civilian

A key ingredient in any survival situation is the mental attitude of the individual involved. — Department of the Army's Field Manual 3-05.70

Whether you've personally made the decision to leave the military or the service has made the decision for you, the clock starts ticking from the moment the decision to transition from military to civilian life is made. Needless to say, it's a BIG step—and survival of this transition starts with you. As with all major changes, preparation is the key.

In the business world, it's called having an "Exit Strategy." What if this product/division/etc. doesn't work out; what are the organization's options? As a service member, you're no different. You need an exit strategy when it comes time for you to leave the service, even though you may get out before your 20 years or retire with 20 or more. Consider it. Plan for it. It's not just for you, it's for your family, too. They also need to see how they're going to fit and transition into the new civilian world.

When is the best time to start preparing for transition? The moment you enter the service. Granted, there's no way to be 100% ready. However, the more prepared you and your family are, the easier the transition will be for everyone. We're making a solid assumption that you want to be prepared; why else would you be reading this book? So in this chapter, we'll focus on getting organized.

Decision Time: Prepare for DABDA

Making a decision regarding your time in the service may not be an easy one, but as with all major life decisions, both voluntary and involuntary (and leaving the service is a major one), there's a high probability that you'll go through a grieving process. As developed by Swiss-born American psychiatrist, Dr. Elisabeth Kubler-Ross, the five stages of grieving include **denial, anger, bargaining, depression**, and **acceptance**. Some people go through each stage in order, while others may skip some stages. Some may get through a stage only to find themselves back in it a later point in grieving process. Whether you take a day to go through it or much longer, we can assure you, it won't be easy.

Why? Because it not only affects you and your immediate family members, but in some situations, it can even reach out to affect your parents, siblings, and extended family. You're connected; it's bound to affect them, some more than others. So, it's better to be aware of the stages of grieving and know that it's a normal but sometimes painful process. Most likely, the grieving process will be more prevalent with an involuntary separation than with a voluntary one, where the person has had more time to think it through and then make a choice.

Let's relate the stages of leaving the military involuntarily and by choice. Here are two real-life examples. The first is a service member, R.V., who was told he is no longer fit for duty, will go through a medical board, and will be medically retired. The second one is a service member, B.L., who recently chosen to retire because his job is getting too hard on his children.

In 2011, R.V. was a 34-year-old ANG Joint Tactical Air Controller (JTAC), attached to an Army Infantry Battalion to Afghanistan that was ambushed by insurgents. An RPG caused him to get blown off a cliff, land on his head, and briefly lose consciousness. He was able to complete his deployment, but upon redeployment he needed multiple surgeries due to his injuries, and began to have symptoms of PTSD and a mild traumatic brain injury (mTBI). It is important to note that R.V. worked as a police officer in his civilian job.

B.L. is a 42-year-old active duty AF Loadmaster/Irregular Warfare SM with 21 years of service. His job requires multiple TDYs and deployments. Although he thoroughly enjoys his work in the military, he's seen how increasingly hard it is on his two young children for him to be gone most of the year. He made a very tough decision to retire from the military to be home for them more often.

Denial, Anger, Bargaining, Depression, Acceptance

Denial. In this stage, the subject may feel in shock, or may be still getting their mind wrapped around the idea that their military career is coming to an end. Maybe a medical condition or family needs have precipitated this decision. No matter the case, it's still hard to believe a decision has been made or an event has occurred that has led to this decision.

R.V. was confident that with a little medical treatment, he would be good to go. He firmly believed he would be going back to JTAC once his medical treatment was done. He hadn't considered the possibility that his condition could potentially make him unfit for military duty *and* jeopardize his civilian job as a police officer. He told us, "I wanted to get whatever surgery I needed to get back to my job. I didn't realize how severe my injuries were, and how significantly they impacted my future in the military. I just thought if I had the surgery, I'd be fixed and ready to go again. Once you're told you're done, the decision is no longer yours, and it takes the wind out of your sails. Any fight you had is lost for the moment. If I thought there was a shot in hell, I would have gone for it. But seeing that I was older, I thought

'What am I fighting for?'. The decision was no longer mine, and it was what it was." After his dedication to being a combat soldier, he didn't want to cross-train as Personnel, which he realized was a just as necessary but less exciting branch of the service.

B.L has his own take on his situation: "It was initially extremely difficult to accept my retirement, in that I still felt I had a lot to offer the ISR/SOF/FID aviation community. I knew the groups would continue on without my involvement... no one is that important. But I still needed the camaraderie, action, adventure and excitement. It's hard to quit that 'cold turkey'."

Anger. Once a person has accepted that there is or will be a loss, they may become angry that the loss has occurred or will be occurring in the near future. They may see it as unjust. Why is this happening to them?

R.V. said this about his anger: "I was always a laidback guy... I wasn't angry until I got hurt. I was able to finish the other seven months of my deployment after I got hurt. But when I returned, the doctor told me I wouldn't be able to continue my job or continue in the military... that made me *very* angry. Picture watching a water glass fall and shatter on the floor... that's how I felt when the doctor was talking to me. I was angry at my unit and leadership when I got hurt. No one contacted my wife when I got hurt. She received *one* phone call from my deployed commander, and that was it. Even in the three years since I got hurt, no one else has contacted my wife. My medical unit, personnel unit, leadership...everyone failed me. It took two years after I returned for someone to step in and say that I would be better being at home getting care versus spending half my week at the unit away from home. And now I retire in February, but my unit has already pushed my retirement ceremony to May...three months after I officially retire. Seriously? Come on. I gave every ounce of my being to this unit and this country. I don't need thanks or a pat on the back... but that unit was my family... they were supposed to be there for me for me... it was all bullshit. I was an asset to the unit, but by God, as soon as you can't do your job, you're done. So yeah, abandoned, let down, pissed off."

B.L. discusses his thoughts: "No real feelings of anger, as I was making the choice for my family's well-being/stability. More disappointment at it all coming to a premature (in my mind) close."

Bargaining. As a last-ditch attempt to recover the loss, the subject may bargain with a "higher being," saying, "I'll behave/stop doing X/get better if I can have it/them back."

R.V. told us, "I don't think I ever bargained. I was angrier than anything. Two middle fingers and a F%$# you."

B.L. didn't go through this stage.

Depression. Once the subject realizes anger and bargaining aren't going to change the outcome and reality sets in, depression may occur. During this phase a person may withdraw, not sleep well, sleep too much, suffer changes in eating habit, and become emotionally fragile. This is compounded when they're also dealing with physical and/or emotional issues that may also be causing depressive symptoms.

R.V. gives his views of depression: "It's hard to know if I can draw the line between my depression related to my PTSD versus my military career ending. Getting blown up, seeing friends die, seeing others with a helpless look when I'm hurt, being told I can't do my job anymore, endless cocktails of medications, poor memory, my head feeling like it's being hit by a hammer, worrying if I injured myself again, switching from being the go-to-guy to a useless relic... a relic because I'm old, a relic because I'm not needed anymore. The medication is a big part of this. A pill for this part of my brain, a pill for my jaw, another for my penis and yet another for my back. Does anyone know how the medications interact? No. As my psychiatrist told me one day, 'Just Google it.'

"The entire process of the VA and military side rating was also a big part. Sitting at night, wondering what the rating will be. If I have a good day at the appointment, will they not rate me the same? What will I get paid? Will it be enough to support me and my family? It's like a big game, and I'm tired of playing games. I'm tired of being worried about everything I say and how that will affect my future."

B.L. shares his "don't quit" attitude the military gives you: "I still had a lot to give, in my mind, and feel I wasn't quite done yet. I don't feel this was depression, but rather the feeling of disappointment—disappointment in myself and disappointment in how I felt... and maybe even a little anger at myself. It's extremely difficult to look your wife, son, and daughter in the eyes and tell them they matter more than anything... as you're eagerly boarding the rotator again to deploy. Gut-wrenching, actually, as I wanted to be back in the air over theater again, dropping supplies and keeping the guys alive for another day... but I knew what made me happy absolutely crushed my family. Guilt might actually describe it best... guilt that I could feel so happy to walk away from those who loved me the most."

Acceptance. The final stage for most of us. The subject has processed all their emotions and has come to accept the reality of what has or is about to occur. Upon reaching acceptance, the subject can move forward with their life.

R.V.: "I've accepted I'm done, and in 47 days I'm going to be Mr. V, Mr. Civilian with my little blue ID card buying vodka at the Class Six. I don't like it at all, and I think that is all I have accepted. You don't take away a 14+ (year) career and say, 'You're done...thanks.' I see all the Vietnam and Korea Vets buying their discount booze and I think, *Is that going to be me in 15 years?*"

B.L.: "The ability to keep all aspects of retirement helped, as it reminded me that *we* were a military family and that *we* had made the choice… not just me. With that, it was just as easy for *us* to transition to civilian life/employment."

What is the takeaway from this? Every person will grieve to some extent. Some are very ready and will have few problems transitioning; others may have a harder time letting go. It's all fine and normal. It only becomes a problem when a person can't get through a stage, leaving them unable to move forward with the rest of their lives.

Mindset: How to Transition from Military to Civilian Life.

Judy Hansen, MA, LPCC, is a licensed therapist in Boulder, CO.[13] She specializes in helping people navigate change in relationships, job and/or location. The following section is her professional advice on ways to transition from a military to civilian mindset.

Anytime a major transition occurs, even if it's welcome, anxiety, fear, and doubt are close companions. Being trained in military protocols means revealing or admitting any kind of vulnerability gives the enemy power. Fear or doubt cannot be revealed in your facial expressions or body language, and it certainly can never be voiced. To do so would invite failure: failure to complete a mission, failure to advance on an enemy, failure to protect those shouldering the fight with you. Those qualities of suppressing your emotions are admirable and necessary to maintain a military operation and mindset of success and accomplishment in that arena. However, those same qualities of self-protection can be harmful, sabotaging and even disastrous in your new civilian life and relationships. This presents a difficult dilemma.

---

[13] http://www.powerforlivingtherapy.com.

On the one hand, you were trained to set aside your emotions, or to compartmentalize fears to be successful in a military operation. On the other hand, in order to succeed in the civilian lifestyle, you must learn to embrace those same emotions, to allow yourself to be more open and vulnerable. In the civilian arena, daring to do so is what creates space for creativity, joy and success. My desire is to reframe what it means to be brave, to fight, to conquer, and how to successfully transition from a military mindset to a civilian one. In both cases, you're a warrior, but you're fighting a different battle, so it requires trading in your weapons for new tools and approaches to problem solving.

Brené Brown, in *Daring Greatly*, explains how being vulnerable is the key to joy, happiness, and fulfillment in life. If we truly want to experience life abundantly, we must learn to be vulnerable. Many of us immediately think, "Heck no! Being vulnerable is what will get me killed. Maybe not literally, but certainly emotionally and professionally!" However, I'm not advocating the "let it all hang out and overshare" approach, like those who make a habit of telling everyone within earshot all their problems and woes. This is not being vulnerable. In truth, it is intended to have the opposite effect. Brené calls that sort of sharing a kind of armor; a way to keep people at a distance. No one can tolerate being around someone like that for long. Instead, we need to be vulnerable by letting those close to us into our struggles so they can support us. She also says as a leader, being vulnerable invites others to authenticity. The following is an example of vulnerability in leadership.

There's some very persuasive leadership research supporting the idea that asking for support is critical, and both vulnerability and courage are contagious. In a 2011 *Harvard Business Review* article, Peter Fuda and Richard Badham use a series of metaphors to explore how leaders spark and sustain change. One of the metaphors is the snowball. The snowball starts rolling when a leader is willing to be vulnerable with his or her subordinates. Their research shows team members predictably perceived this act of vulnerability as courageous. It inspires others to follow suit. Supporting the metaphor of the snowball is the story of Clynton, the managing director of a large German corporation who realized his directive leadership style was preventing senior managers from taking initiative.

The researchers explain, "He could have worked in private to change his behavior—but instead he stood up at an annual meeting of his top sixty managers, acknowledged his failings, and outlined both his personal and organizational roles. He admitted that he didn't have all of the answers and asked his team for help leading the company." Having studied Clynton's transformation, the researchers report his effectiveness surged, his team flourished, increases in initiative and innovation were noted, and his organization went on to outperform much larger competitors.[14]

Brown goes on to say, "Connection is why we're here. We are hardwired to connect with others, it's what gives us purpose and meaning to our lives, and without it there is suffering,"[15] and "Vulnerability is the core, the heart, the center, of meaningful human experiences."[16]

So if we're hardwired for connection, and if vulnerability is the key to our happiness, how does that translate to being successful as a civilian in the workplace or at home? What does this transition look like? The following are a few simple steps to make that transition.

Ceasefire. Make peace with your military experience. Whether forced or voluntary, clear your mind of any resentment, anger or bitterness. If at all possible, forgive in person and let go of any need to

---

[14] *Daring Greatly* by Brené Brown, p. 54
[15] *Ibid,* p. 8.
[16] *Ibid,* p. 12.

retaliate. This will set you free to re-engage in new and healthy relationships. If you skip this step, you will persist in carrying negative emotional baggage and it will continue to hurt you and others, hampering your future success.

Declaration. Make the declaration that you will be thankful for your military experiences and appreciate how those will soon translate into a positive future for you. There's something powerful about having a grateful heart. It changes brainwaves; it makes hard things easier to bear; and, it creates a positive outlook on life. In *The Happiness Advantage,* Shawn Achor asserts by keeping a list of "three good things" that happen each day, "your brain will be forced to scan the last 24 hours for potential positives—things that brought small or large laughs, feelings of accomplishment at work, a strengthened connection with family, a glimmer of hope for the future. In just five minutes a day, this trains the brain to become more skilled at noticing and focusing on possibilities for personal and professional growth, and seizing opportunities to act on them."[17] In doing so, "we become more successful when we are happier and more positive."[18] All this adds up to creating an environment inviting to others who are positive into your circle of influence, helping you succeed. As you engage in your new career with gratefulness and positivity, you will be on your way to living the life of your dreams.

Don't go AWOL. You might be tempted to check out of all the hard work it might take to reengage in civilian life. There is much less discipline imposed on you in the civilian world, so now you must become the leader of your new life's mission and create your new career. You might decide all this "vulnerability" crap is for sissies and children, but it isn't for you. You might want to numb it all out with your drug of choice, such as working long hours, alcoholism or even

---

[17] Shawn Achor, *The Happiness Advantage,* p. 100, e-book version.
[18] Achor, p. 15.

addiction to prescription medication. You may be tempted to avoid fully living in the present. Our challenge to you is, "Don't give up, and don't give in!" When you finally push through to the other side, you will find the fight was worth the freedom you now feel.

Objective. You need to have your "Next Step" identified so you can move in this planned direction. Your Next Step or Steps can then reveal to you what your "Next Mission" in life is going to be. You can then pursue your next mission with all the alacrity and gusto instilled in you. It's about exploring new options, not about having everything perfect. Success is never a straight line. It has many twists and turns. Be true to yourself and trust your process. When you reflect upon each step, you will see the natural progression. This is not to imply there won't be unanticipated challenges along the way. Having a Plan A starts you in the direction, but we also recommend having a Plan B and Plan C, and above all else, to keep going forward on your new path.

Getting Organized

There are three areas that apply whether you're in the military service or in the business world: know where you are, know where you're going, and define the steps to get there. The same principles can be applied to transitioning from military to civilian life.

Know Who and Where You Are

It can be difficult to take a hard look at your situation and see where you truly stand. Who doesn't want to believe they're okay? It's too easy to assume and then find out down the road (and possibly too late) that this isn't the case. Bottom line, you must take a hard, honest look. It's critical to know exactly where you currently are to be able to figure out your options. Here are areas we recommend you examine before making future-impacting decisions.

31

Family.

Don't forget about your family; they're transitioning as well. Ensure you include them in all your decisions, from where you're going to live, to what schools they'll go to, to financial issues, medical issues, etc. Your spouse may need to get a new job in a new place.

If you're single and have no family depending on you, your decisions are yours to make. Of course, even single people have significant people in their lives (e.g. parents, friends, or a partner) whose wishes may need to be considered. We'll never say these decisions are easy; no major life decision ever is.

If do you have a family, we recommend talking openly with them. Knowing their thoughts and desires will weigh in on your approach. Some topics you may want to talk about include:

Spouse/Partner
1. Do you agree on where you want to put down roots?
2. Is this a final move?
3. Does he/she have a job they want to/can leave?
4. Is your partner in school? Will they graduate or transfer schools?
5. Do they want to start school?
6. Do they have medical needs that warrant specific care?

Kids
1. Are they near graduation?
2. Do they want to go to college near home?
3. Do you want them to stay put or do they want to stay put until high school graduation?
4. Do they have preferences on where they want to live?
5. Do they have medical needs that warrant special care?

Other Family Members
1. Do elderly family members has special medical needs?
2. Nursing home: are they moving to a new nursing home to be near you?
3. Living with you: can they handle a move?

Having these discussions isn't always easy, but it's extremely important to allow everyone to know where each person's thoughts are regarding the transition. Some may be happy with the current set-up and not ready to have anything change. Others may be ready for a change and look forward to moving. There's no way to make everyone completely happy. However, ensuring everyone is on the same page allows for everyone to prepare, in their own way, for an upcoming change. Furthermore, doing it together allows those having a harder time to lean on their family for support.

When B.L. decided it was time to retire, he had many discussions with his spouse. They had two young children (7 and 3-1/2). His wife had been in her job for just over 1-1/2 years and she did not want to quit her work. Their oldest had just started elementary in a good school he son liked. They did not have any family living near them, and even though their parents lived in other states, they were healthy and lived independently.

When they looked at their situation, they determined that with one spouse in a solid job, it gave B.L. time to look around at his options in the local area. Even if he didn't get a job before he got out, they would still be financially stable.

And speaking of finances… that's another critical area to consider.

Finances
As soon as you know you're going to separate or retire, you need to get your finances organized. Yes, it can be hard, but it's imperative

to know how much you will need to cushion you through transition (which may include relocating), and how much you will need to make in the civilian sector to cover your living expenses. Military pay does not transition to civilian pay dollar-for-dollar, and the value of your dollar will vary depending on your location. There is a lot to take into consideration, such as:

- The cost of living where you're going to live.
- State and other taxes.
- Healthcare benefits (critical to know if you're separating or receiving severance pay).
- Bonus/commissions.
- Investment options (matching 401K).

"Start saving money and investing for the future. No one told me this when I was a young E4, getting married. Soon there were three kids, and saving money became hard. I have the discipline to do it now, but had I started earlier, I would be in a much better financial position to do what I want rather than doing what I need to do to get to what I want." *B.O., CMS(ret), Senior Engineer, 36 years USA & ANG.*

A great place to start is your branch of service's Military and Family Readiness Office. They will assist you in looking at your current income, future income, current bills, future bills, budget, and assist with developing a financial pathway.

Air Force Airmen and Family Readiness
https://www.usafservices.com/

Air Force Reserve Family Program
http://www.afrc.af.mil/library/airmanfamilyreadiness/index.asp

Army Family Readiness Group
https://www.armyfrg.org/skins/frg/home.aspx

Army Reserve Family Program
http://www.arfp.org

Navy Fleet and Family Readiness (also serves Reserves)
http://www.cnic.navy.mil/ffr/family_readiness.html

Marine Command Family Readiness Program
http://www.marcorsyscom.marines.mil/CommandStaff/Family
ReadinessOfficer(FRO).aspx

Marine Forces Reserve Family Program
https://www.manpower.usmc.mil/portal/page/portal/M_RA_H
OME/MF/Personal%20and%20Professional%20Development/
C_PFMP

The Office of the Secretary of Defense (OSD) has a Regular Military Compensation Calculator at http://militarypay.defense.gov/mpcalcs/Calculators/RMC.aspx. Key in on the word "regular." This is a good calculator to figure out what your basic compensation is (base pay, BAH, with/without dependents, state tax). It does *not* include extra money you were getting from deployment, incentive pay, or bonuses for critically manned career fields. For example, if you have dependents and deployed annually, you may need to take into account the tax-free, hazard duty, imminent danger, hostile fire, and family separation pay. If you were on special duty status (diver, flight crew, parachute, flight deck, demolition) you would need to take into account the extra monthly pay you received.

Once you've added up all pay and studied your budget, you will have a much better idea of what you will need for a successful transition.

You may also have another resource to tap for assistance. The Wounded Warrior Program for each branch can assist and/or guide you in the right direction for organizing your finances. You can find the link for each branch in Chapter 4: "You're Injured, Now What?"

As we stated earlier, knowing your financial status will help you decide the next steps. Do you want to work full time, part time, or volunteer? Do you want to go back to school to change career directions? Are you interested in starting your own business? Knowing your financial status will allow you to decide how and when you can pursue your passion. Maybe you have debt you need to clear before going back to school or opening your business. It might be better to work a full-time job for a specified period of time to allow you to clear your debt before potentially creating more. For those choosing to separate, after taking a hard look at your finances and budget, you may realize it's not financially a good time to separate. On the other hand, maybe you'll find it's a perfect time; you'll be able to cover all your expenses and are able to go to school, start a business, or volunteer your time. Either way, knowing your financial health will allow you to plan appropriately.

You may be thinking there's no way of knowing all the variables until you get to that point. For example, if you're going through a medical board, you may not know your military and veteran disability rating until 3-4 months before your discharge from the service. Or, if you're filing a VA claim, it will be months (or a year or more) before the claim is processed. Yes, they're the unknown factors—but not completely unknown. This is where your branch's Family Readiness Centers or Wounded Warrior liaisons are trained and can assist with looking at those variables.

We interviewed a retired colonel and a current financial advisor who both assist service members and veterans with setting up financial pathways to allow them to fulfill personal and family goals. Here is their advice:

We know financial planning is very individual and takes in a lot of variables for a successful formula. But the fundamental basics are the same. We know many of you are on a solid financial path. Excellent! In that case, the following information will be more of a refresher than knowledge to implement. For others, this may be new information... so feel free to use it as a stepping stone to your financial future. And don't stress if you feel you're starting late in the proverbial game. You're starting, and that's what counts.

Joining the military started you on one of life's journeys that, at some point in the future, will come to an end with separation or retirement. Many of us start our military service knowing we'll be in the service for a short span of time, such as one enlistment, or a period that covers a commitment for education, training, etc. Some may know they're in for the long haul and plan on retiring from the military. Others may not be sure, and stay for more than one or two tours before separating. On occasion, separation occurs that we haven't planned for (e.g. force drawdowns, RIFs). One thing for sure is one day, we won't wear the uniform to work.

You learn quickly in the military there are plans for everything. Big plans for fighting a war; mobility plans for getting there; logistic plans for sustaining the force; and so on, right down to a plan for hosting local community leaders. At the core of all these plans is understanding a plan helps us determine an objective, organize our resources, and implement logical steps to achieve our objectives. It's a roadmap from here to there.

We each know our military career is finite, be it programmed for a single enlistment or more than 20 years. It will end, and not always on our terms. So let's develop our personal finances to handle the transition back to civilian life.

When do you plan for transition?

Ask yourself the question, "When is the best time to plant a tree?" If you want shade now, take the steps before the sun is at its brightest. Planning for transition is like planting a tree. Starting early allows you to reap the benefits later. You can't turn back the clock, but you can start now.

There are a ton of unknowns in your future. What will the economy be like when you separate/retire? Will you be single or married? Will you have dependents? Where will you want to live and work? How much will it cost to get established? Will your future employer cover costs? How about education and GI educational benefits?

That's a lot of questions to think about! Let's organize the information and start to lay the foundation for your inevitable transition.

Elements of Your Financial Plan

Cash. Let's plant that tree early in your military career by starting with a savings plan. How, you ask? Simple: pay yourself first. Make sure you have an allotment going into reserve to handle the unexpected big emergencies (that hopefully do not happen), <u>AND</u> the transition back to the civilian world.

Some of you may be asking, "Why not use my checking account?" Because checking accounts tend to be what we use to live on, covering our day-to-day expenses. If any dollars are left at the end of the month, there's a tendency to spend the remaining money on something. If you separate the dollars into a second location, they become "special" and are more likely to be there when needed and wanted. Remember, water and money have a physical characteristic in common: exposed to air, both tend to evaporate.

Now you may be wondering, "How much should go into this pot?" Can you develop an amount that is absolutely accurate down to the last penny? Well, that depends. Someone retiring and getting a retirement check has a better idea of their transitional income versus the person who is separating; so maybe you can't make a guess at the start, but you do need to start.

A rule of thumb is to sock away about 5% of your pre-tax compensation. This is where the allotment comes into play. Let's put away that 5% before you have a chance to miss it. Now the question is "How long do I keep the allotment going?" There are, of course, many variables according to your goals (full-time versus part-time school, starting a business, just taking a break). However, another rule of thumb is to build up approximately 3-6 months of pay and allowances. You may want a bigger nest egg, if you think or know you will be without an income for a longer period of time.

Finance Tip: If you've calculated what you're currently earning and know approximately what you'll earn as a civilian, scale back your spending months or years in advance of retirement, and put your savings into your bank accounts so you can start living as if you're a civilian, and so that it won't shock the family's spending habits when you get out. Spreading out the many changes that will occur over time will lessen the stress when the time comes to get out.

Investments. Beyond savings, it's wise to invest for the "big ticket" expenses/needs you'll face in life. Think retirement income, a home purchase, education, weddings, vacations, religious missions, opening a business, etc. How much? Another rule-of-thumb answer: about 10% percent of your pre-tax income should go into investments.

Security/Insurance Considerations. This isn't always a fun topic to discuss, but it's an important one. Like the overall financial plan, insurance needs are specific to the individual. Below is a list of the various insurances and benefits available to the service member.

1) **Serviceman's Group Life Insurance (SGLI)** offers secure coverage for service members and dependents at low/no costs.
2) **Dependency Indemnification Compensation (DIC)** and **Active Duty Services Benefit Program (ASBP)** provide monthly payments for all survivors of an active duty member who dies. The length of payment varies.
3) **Dependents Educational Assistance** can be available if death occurs on active duty.
4) **Death Gratuity** is available if the service member dies on active duty.
5) **Social Security benefits** for survivors is available whether death occurs on active duty or not.

Altogether, the active duty survivor benefits can easily have an equivalent life insurance value of over $1 million for a military family. When we retire or separate, they "stay inside the gate" after a brief carry-over period.

Should insurance be a consideration on active duty? After all, the military provides coverage while we're in; why get more? Well, here's something to consider: the younger you are, the cheaper the life insurance. The earlier you lock it in, the less you pay in premiums. A look into future needs is beneficial. The better we are at evaluating our permanent long term needs, the less we'll need to spend.

For example, $100,000 of coverage with Veteran's Group Life Insurance (VGLI) is available to separated/retired service members. Currently SGLI goes to $400,000. Do the math.

Age	Coverage	Monthly
40	$100,000	$17.00
60-64	$100,000	$108.00
70-74	$100,000	$225.00
over 75	$100,000	$450.00

Another factor with life insurance covers insurability. If you're relatively young and healthy, insurance companies charge you less. Also, a future profession may limit your ability to purchase life insurance.

Beyond life insurance, there are property and casualty requirements, such as home-owners, vehicle, boat, and renter's insurance. These needs may well apply both while on active duty and after the military.

Health insurance is covered on active duty. If you retire or are medically retired with a rating of 30% or greater, you're eligible to continue to receive Tricare; and once you reach the age of 65, you will have a combination of Tricare and Medicare.

Got the wheels turning? Hope so! It's important to make sure all the angles are covered. So the question is, what is the right amount? You want to be covered, but not insurance-poor. Save about 5% percent for those identified permanent needs.

It's a lot of information! Saving, investments, insurance—and we haven't even talked nuts-and-bolts, nitty-gritty stuff for the transition back to the civilian street yet. But when you step back and think about it, if you have a big-picture plan in place and have been monitoring it along the way, then getting down into the weeds at the 18-month, 12-month, six-month, and three-month points can be a lot more comfortable and, more importantly, doable. You're able to approach being "one of them" (a.k.a. a civilian) again with a lot more confidence if you know you have enough to allow you to make the best choices for you and your dependents when you consider your work/education/volunteer/passion, locations, etc.

Now that you're armed with all this knowledge, it's a perfect time to develop a workable financial plan for yourself and dependents. You do not need a degree in finance to have a plan. You can get help both on- and off-base. Once you make a good plan, keep it running at current levels, and it can work for a lifetime.

The Transition. Let's get into to the nuts and bolts as you go from the abstract (someday) to the specific (retirement in 84 days). First if you haven't already done so, develop a monthly budget. Why? So you know what it costs to live today.

Income

Income	Item	Amount
Base Pay	Base Pay	
	Housing	
	Clothing	
Specialty Pay	Flight	
	Bonuses	
	Hazard Duty	
	Combat Pay	
Second Job		
Spouse Income		
	Sub Totals	
Deductions	Federal Taxes	
	State Taxes	
	SSDI	
	Medicare	
	Totals	

Expenses

Expense	Item	Amount
Housing	Rent/Mortgage	
	Utilities	
	Insurance	
Food		
Transportation		
Health Care		
Insurance		
Entertainment (Cable, date night, bowling leagues, etc.)		
Education		
Credit Cards		
Loans (Auto, furniture, equity, etc.)		
Savings		
Investments		
	Totals	

Subtract expenses from income. The difference, if positive, can provide some additional resource for the transitional budget, if needed.

When establishing a projected budget for the civilian world, remember to include:

- Health Insurance.
- State and local taxes that may not have applied on active duty.
- Other monthly costs as known/projected based on local averages.
- Total Income, including:
  o Retirement pay
  o VA compensation
  o Future Salary
  o Spouse Salary

If the total projected income equals or exceeds the projected expenses, then cheer! If not, develop a priority list from the monthly budget and defer or eliminate the nice but non-critical items until you reach a balance.

This is all good if you have a job and a known destination, but what if you just got orders for "not-ever-going-there" base and the fun meter is pegged? You don't have it in you and you're ready to separate. For Guard and Reserve, moving/commuting may or may not be required. However, for any component, are you ready for the loss of income?

Time to look at your current budget and bounce it against that savings/money market account you started and see how long you're self-sustainable. Is it long enough for a decent job search in the area you prefer? If so, decide if burning a bridge or two is worth saying your piece and dropping your papers.

If not, can you add enough from current excess in the timeframe allotted? If you can, all the above applies. If not, maybe you need to sign on for another tour and get that plan going.

When you don't have a choice and a mandatory retirement or separation is upon you…budget, budget, budget. Identify the "must pays" and cut the rest now. If you're in the negative, check savings and build up as much as you can; check investments and identify a withdrawal priority for future implementation. If it's still not enough, ask Mom about the room in the basement.

Okay: a lot of information to process. To get you started, at the end of the book there's a detailed checklist to use when setting up your budget. When you have a chance, give this section a reread. But if you don't/can't/are unable to, at least remember these key points.

- We all want to separate or retire, and most do.
- If you pay ourselves first, over a long period of time, you improve your ability for a stress-free termination.
- Developing and using a real-life budget on active duty will make it easier to adjust and plan for the transition's implementation. You can choose the best option, not just take the first available.
- The best plan isn't necessarily the one with the fanciest and most charts and graphs. It's one that fits you and that you understand.
- Don't be afraid to ask for help. Very few people know your job. There are resources available on and off base.

You: Skills Testing to Part-Time Work.

Loves, Likes, Dislikes, and Skills. Now that you have talked with your family and taken a hard look at your financial health, the next step is about you. It's about finding out what your talents and interests are. You've been in the military for a long time, and have done many things you found you enjoyed, and most likely many others you didn't enjoy so much. However, whether you liked it or not, you built a set of skills that the military needed. Now it's time to give all those skills a name, combine them with your talents and passion, and make your next employment take-off.

46

Quantifying all those skills can be a difficult task. As one service member stated when asked what his skills were: "I take orders and shoot the bad guy." Okay, but the average job fair doesn't have a lot of recruiters for "sniper." He had to get more specific. After some discussion, he was able to communicate his ability to critically think under pressure, make accurate decisions in split-seconds, rapidly prioritize, demonstrate excellent communication and people skills, maintain a very detailed-oriented approach, and he knew how to utilize available resources to get a job done.

Transitioning from the military to civilian life is about reframing what you did into words and images the average civilian will understand. You translate the military details, terms, acronyms, and some mindsets and thinking into a broader sense and terms. Most have at least heard the term "looking from the 30,000-foot view," even if we may not have had jobs requiring it. The idea is you move from the ground level of being a technician (infantry, pilot, sniper, cook) up to the 30,000-foot level (from specific details to general concepts) and then cross from the military territory and terminology over the military/civilian boundary into civilian territory. Write and talk as civilians might see it, not as service members see it.

Simply put, you now have to look at the civilian big picture and how you fit into it. It's about thinking higher up the process chain, from details to tactics to strategy to ideas and concept, and changing the process terms to tell or sell others about your skills and talents. While most understand the "culture clash" surrounding visiting a foreign country, it applies equally when visiting an Air Force base when you're in the Navy or interviewing for work at Apple or Microsoft. The better you are at speaking their "civilianese" and understanding their culture, the better you will be at getting work. The term "you're overqualified" means they don't feel comfortable with you. Being "comfortable" means many things to them, like will you yell for someone to get you a cup of coffee?

If you're having a hard time figuring out your skills, have no fear, there are resources available to assist. The American Job Center Network (http://jobcenter.usa.gov/) is a central nexus of collective information for everything occupation-related, from the Department of Education, Department of Labor, Department of Veteran Affairs, General Services Administration, Small Business Association and even the White House. Even though it's centralized, there's a lot of information to look through. If you prefer to talk directly to someone, you can enter your zip code and find a Workforce Solutions location near you. To get you started, we've sifted through all the information and pulled out websites that are specific to assisting you in finding your post military dream mission.

My Next Move for Veterans
(http://www.mynextmove.org/vets) allows you to plug in your AFSC/MOS/Rating under "I liked my last job," whereupon it will list the skills associated with that military job. You can also browse various careers by industry or put in key words to describe your dream job and get a list of careers that match the key words.

Career One Stop (http://www.careeronestop.org/) is a wealth of information. Try out the Skills Profiler at http://www.careerinfonet.org/skills/default.aspx?nodeid=20. Interested in seeing the civilian jobs that match closest to your military job? Then Check out the Veteran Re-Employment link (http://www.careeronestop.org/ReEmployment/veterans/defaul t.aspx).

What if you don't even know what you're interested in? Well, there are online resources available to assist you with that also. The **Occupational Informational Network (O*Net)** was developed by the Department of Labor/Employment and Training Administration to be the nation's primary source of occupational information. The O*Net Interest Profiler (http://www.mynextmove.org/explore/ip) has 60 questions on various work activities. Questions are to be answered without regard to how the job pays or how skilled a person currently is. The goal is to get a base line of your interests.

Testing and Assessment. The books *Now Discover Your Strengths* by Marcus Buckingham and *Strength Finder 2.0* by Tom Rath offer online tests that give you your top five areas of strengths that will help you narrow down where you should focus your future time and efforts looking for work.

Kevin: The Strength Finder test nailed what my talents are and what I love to do. My wife found out upon taking her test that she was right in the career she was supposed to be in, too. Many of my friends in the startup community refer to their results from this test to compare notes and skills, as well as keep an eye out for people who are needed with skills that they're weak in.

Generally, most individuals have an idea of what they enjoyed doing when they were young, so sometimes even what you learned as a young person gives you an insight into what areas you have the best chance of being successful. But other times you find you might try something you've never had a chance to try and find out you rather like it. Of primary importance: We all have multiple talents, and it's important you find ALL of the talents you enjoy, and find work that need your talents and strengths. After all, we only have one shot at this life; might as well make it one you wake up every day looking forward to living.

Okay, you've done the work and found your interests. Now: what do you do with that information?

Investigate. There are a lot of assessments you can take. However, assessments will only get you so far. Once you're able to determine work/jobs/careers matching your talents and passions, it's important to do a little investigating. Just because an assessment says you have an interest in helping people doesn't mean you have to sign up for medical school. You may also put an emphasis on things like spending quality time with your family, stable hours, and your tendency to nearly pass out at the sight of blood… all of which aren't compatible with many medical field careers. However, there are many other avenues that could work. Explore your options!

List potential industries. Make a list of all the industries and career fields that help people. Look at their skills and see if they match yours, and if not, how much training it will take to get you to that level. Ask yourself if you're willing and/or able to get the training required.

Network and talk with others. Go talk to people working in that area. Ask questions. What do they like best/least about the job? What are the hours like? Is there flexibility? What are some things they didn't expect, good or bad, when they entered the career field? Take it a step further and volunteer time. The benefit is twofold. First, you get to see if you enjoy the work; if there are parts that are better or worse than you expected; if there are requirements that you were unaware of; and whether the work environment is compatible to you. Lastly, you're telling the place you're working that you're serious about learning and gaining more experience in the field. If a job becomes available, the person who volunteered time and was already trained by the employer most likely has the best shot at the job.

Donna: A co-worker of mine is getting ready to retire in a couple months. He has been actively looking for a post-military retirement job and decided to volunteer time at a non-profit. He really likes the people and he felt very rewarded by the work he was doing. He decided to talk to the staff about job openings, and is now pursuing full-time work with them.

Trial and error. Having narrowed down what you think you'd like to do, the next step is to actually try out the industry, career, or work you're interested in.

Volunteering. If you can't find part-time work, volunteer. Even volunteering for an organization keeps your "service mindset" intact as a veteran, and it also gives you the opportunity, if no part-time work is available, to get your foot into the door.

Part-time work. Apply for part-time work in the industry or career that interests you. So what if it's below your pay grade for a while? You get to see, from the bottom looking up, what's happening and whether or not you'd like to be a part of it. *And* you get paid for learning the job.

Kevin: I consulted with a soon-to-be-retired Lockheed Martin employee; he wanted to open a bakery with his life savings. I asked him if he had worked in a bakery before. He said, "No," but he could not be swayed and went ahead and invested his retirement money—and then preceded to close his shop six months after he started. Instead, he should have volunteered or gotten an entry level job in the area he wanted to work in. If, after six months, he was still loving it, then he could have taken the next step. Either he could have moved up into a better-paying position with the bakery, or gone out on his own. Take some time to do the work first, before you invest a considerable amount of time and effort choosing something new.

I also had a talk with a young lady who did "hair and nails," as she put it. When asked what she really loved to do as a young girl, she said she loved animals. Long story short, I suggested volunteering at the local veterinarian for a few hours a month or getting a job at a pet store to see if she still had an interest, and then narrow down what she liked and disliked about working with animals. If she disliked the medical aspect, she could have tried pet grooming or training.

Know Where You're Going

There is no changing the fact that your days in the military are numbered. Whether you make the decision yourself or external forces lead to separating/retiring from your branch of service, it will be a tough day, both for you and your family. It will be a significant, life-changing event that will affect everyone in your family and maybe even your extended family. Making the decision to leave gives rise to a new question (and the whole purpose of this book): **What now?**

Donna: I'm going to digress here for a minute to hopefully make a point. We watch a lot of Disney-Pixar in the Hoffmeyer household, and right now we're heavily into princesses, courtesy of our 3½ year old daughter. Needless to say, that makes us involuntary experts in all princess movies. In the movie *Tangled* there's a scene where Rapunzel and Flynn are in a tavern filled with thieves and murderers. At one point, the thieves and murders break out in song and dance regarding the perception they put out (big, mean, and scary) as opposed to what they dreamed of being (a concert pianist, for example).

(If you're not familiar with the movie, it's worth a watch… even if you don't have children. We won't say anything, promise.)

These thugs decided to use the raw skills they had, even if they didn't completely enjoy it. Although they still had deep-down desires they wanted to fulfill, they didn't for one reason or another. (I'm guessing this guy's hook limited his job prospects for concert pianist.)

By no means are we categorizing you with thugs! The point here is we all have dreams; and sometimes, for whatever reason, we get on a different path and end up doing something we have skills in, but it isn't really our passion. Donna has a knack for grammar, but by no means does she have any desire to be an editor. It's important to have as clear an idea of the direction you want to go in when you leave active duty. Are you just going to take the first available job? (We really hope not!) Are you going to advance your education? (Okay, first available job to support yourself through school is understandable.) However, finding a job to enhance your knowledge in your desired field is even better. Are you looking to work at a small business? Perhaps a position in a large corporation is more familiar and comfortable. Are you going to stay in the same line of work or go a completely different direction? Are you going to go into business for yourself? Are you going to take the big plunge and follow your dream? (Which could involve any of the above scenarios, or perhaps a combination.)

This is a good place to stop and put all this information into context of *passion*. After all, that's the main reason we're writing this book. "Passion" is defined by the Oxford Dictionary as "an intense desire or enthusiasm for something." Sit in a quiet place when you have a few moments and let your mind wander. What did you want to be when you were a kid? Teenager? Young Adult? If location, money and benefits weren't a factor, what would you be doing? This is where you ask yourself, "What is it that excites me? What would I wake up and want to do every day, whether I got paid or not?"

Have that image in your mind? You may be surprised what that image was 20/30/40 years ago; it may not be the same thing as it is today. Then again, maybe it is. Did you put aside something you loved to do because it didn't pay the bills? Maybe you even joined the military out of needs-must versus desire.

Donna: A technician who used to work with me had a gift for writing and theater. She was very expressive, creative and articulate. She simply lit up when she talked about the arts. I always scratched my head about why she chose to come into the military. Don't get me wrong, she was an excellent medical technician: extremely smart, organized and skilled at her job. But I could tell this really wasn't her true desire, and she was just doing it for something to do. Scroll ahead, and she gets married and gets out of the military. She and her spouse have two children and she goes back to school for accounting. What?! I was confused and I asked why accounting? She was such a gifted writer, after all. She told me that writing didn't pay the bills and take care of the family. Okay, I understood that, but was bummed she wasn't pursuing her true love of the arts.

Scroll ahead again, and she is now divorced and decided the safest choice is for her to come back to the military as Medical Service Officer. I didn't ask why this time; I understood, but was still saddened she had to make this choice. One final hop to the present... life has thrown her some curve balls, and she is now in process of being medically boarded. However, as a result, she has had to take a hard look at what she wants to do when she takes off the uniform for good. She just started volunteering at a Senior Center, teaching creative writing. She loves working with her new students so much that she is now considering pursuing a degree in social work and specializing in working with senior citizens who need assistance.

Keep in mind, all these assessments may show you would be a great fit in one area, but do not have a huge interest in that area. Maybe you score strong in art, but it's not something you enjoy. Instead, you've always loved fixing up cars. Maybe you've just done it as a weekend hobby on cars you fixed by reading the Chilton's Manual and through trial and error. But it's the one thing that makes you smile and excited to do.

Be creative! Think out of the box! Maybe you can use your artistic mind to create custom designs for cars. Custom-painted steering wheel, anyone? This is a second chance to go for that dream job, whether it's starting your own business, working for a business, or volunteering. If you're retiring, you have a small financial compensation as a cushion. Whether you're retiring or separating, are you building a nest egg to fall back on while you pursue your next mission? If not, is postponing retirement or separation for a year or two an option? If it isn't, what changes can you make to your budget to enable you to save income? This is where your branch of service family readiness center or a financial advisor can assist you. Being as financially secure as possible will allow you to pursue what you DESIRE! (Refer back to the earlier part of this chapter.)

Let's take a look at the options.

Guard and Reserve

Joining the Reserves and or the National Guard may be an option for you to continue your service and not lose any of the skills or time and experience you've acquired over the last few years. This is one of the first questions you need to ask yourself, as this will give you several options to continue to connect and utilize your skill set to continue to serve your country.

Donna: I separated from ADAF after 12 years, took 4 years off, and then came back to the Reserves when we moved to San Antonio. Here are some tips from personal experience:

Start early. The administrative process isn't speedy. I was brought on to the Reserves in June and my first drill weekend was September... and that was with the Chief Nurse pushing the process along. Find out all the reserve/guard units in the state you're moving to and see what their mission is.

Be willing to cross-train or travel. The closest unit to you may not have your area of specialty. Recruiters and your resume are not as effective as a face-to-face meeting with the person running the day-to-day operations of the unit (FYI, this is usually not the commander). Yes, you have to go through the recruiters for the administrative process, but meeting face-to-face allows the unit to get to know you the person, not you the piece of paper. If the unit's interested in you, they will set up and interview with you. We recommend being proactive. Try to see if it's a fit for you before formally engaging a recruiter.

Go to a drill weekend, talk to the unit members and meet the leadership. For the outsider it will look chaotic, but there's a method to the madness. It just takes time to get the flow. If you decide you're interested, then go and talk to a recruiter. There's a good chance they'll love you, since you did the hard work for them and found yourself a Reserve/Guard home.

A last tip: Everyone who leaves active duty is required to do a specified period of Inactive Ready Reserves (IRR), usually two years. However, if you think you may want to come back to the military after the specified IRR time, you may want to ask to stay on IRR status. It will make coming back to the military a little quicker administratively. Check with the Reserve or Guard recruiter for your specific branch of service for most current information regarding IRR:

- Army Reserves (usar.army.mil)
- Navy Reserves (navyreserve.com)

- Air Force Reserves (afreserve.com)
- Marine Reserves (www.marforres.marines.mil)
- Coast Guard (www.uscg.mil/reserves)

Public Life: Local, State, and Federal Government

If joining the Reserve/Guard is no longer an option but you want to continue your mission to further serve your country, another option is joining the public sector as a government employee. You'll get to capitalize on your time in the military as "time served" through various veteran preferences. Check out your local, state and our federal government for opportunities to continue your service. Here is a list to get you started:

Organization	Website
American Job Center	jobcenter.usa.gov
Feds Hire Vets	fedshirevets.gov
My Career @ VA	mycareeratva.va.gov
VA for Vets	vaforvets.va.gov
USA Jobs	usajobs.gov
NAFJOBS	nafjobs.org
Army Civilian Service	armycivilianservice.com
VEPO	dm.usda.gov/employ/vepo/index.htm

Civilian Life: Corporate, Business, or Entrepreneur?

For some, leaving active duty may not mean leaving the military entirely. They may decide to continue with the Guard or Reserves, to maintain a source of income, while pursuing civilian endeavors (e.g. school, entrepreneurship, or a new career path).

Corporate. While Fortune 500 companies may be close in size to military commands, with tens of thousands of employees, they also have similar "big company processes" like the military does. This translates into long lead times for making decisions, and means finding work in one of their many departments.

Finding work in a large corporation isn't much different than working for the military; you have large numbers of steps to go through to get a decision made for you to start work. The larger the business is, the longer it might take to get hired. You might need to take a part-time job or start a side business until something larger takes.

Business—Full Time or Part Time. The smaller the business, the quicker a decision can be made, but the smaller the budget is for pay and other items like benefits.

Full time. Working full time is what most choose to do before leaving the service, but it may not be the ideal end result for you and your family. It could be a stepping-stone to your dream areas of work.

Part time. Working part time may not be your first choice. But by earning while you're learning, you can see firsthand whether you like the organization and/or the work. This can be especially true if you and your family decide to try the next step, entrepreneurship. Working part time in an industry that you want to open a business in gives you some insights into what it takes to run it. You can also learn what you like and dislike about the industry and where you would like to work and what you would do the same or differently in your business. It's an opportunity to get an "insider's look" at how things are done.

Entrepreneurship. If you want to strike out on your own, the best advice is "Start now!"—while you're in the service. Don't wait until you get out of the service to start your own company. There's never is a "right time" to start a business. Starting a business while you're in the service not only builds up your business acumen, but also any potential

58

profits can go into your savings or be plowed back to grow your business while you're still enjoying the security of a military paycheck. It also gives your spouse and the rest of your family a look into what it would take to succeed in the civilian marketplace, and provides you some business experience.

This can be especially helpful when your whole family gets involved. Your spouse might initially have never considered starting a business of their own, but supporting and helping you in your quest for a new stream of income or career beginning might squelch any fear they might have and give them hope that they, too, could strike out on their own.

Search for success, then scale. The best advice is to start small and make small mistakes rather than plunging any life savings, retirement funds or borrowing large sums at the start. Small mistakes mean small costs, until you find the right formula for business success. Go big only if you have success. You can think big, but you don't go big until you're successful at selling to regular and steady customers at a profit. In other words, don't jump out of the plane until you're confident your chute will work.

Starting a business while you're still in the service means you can continue your business on the side while working for a corporation or a small business. The key issue for you and your family is to have multiple streams of income, because you never know what the market will do at any point. You may get laid off, or your business may go downhill; prepare for both. If one income stream dries up, you have others to help. Leaving the military means you now have to take more responsibility for yourself and your family. That means keeping your opportunity eyes open to earning income and taking care of your family. Even if you do find work in the public sector, you can start a business based on your talents and passions that could involve the whole family.

Action Plan: Create a Plan

- Where You Are
  - Family Input
  - Finances – can I afford it?
    - Debt
    - Savings
  - Define your capabilities
    - Skills
    - Likes
    - Dislikes
- Where You're Going
  - Education
    - Certification
    - Degree/Advance Degree
  - Military
    - Guard/Reserves
- Government Employee
- Corporate
- Business
- Entrepreneurship
- Volunteer work
- Steps to Get There
  - Financial Planning
  - Determine Your Path
    - Education Assistance
    - Small Business Planning
    - Start Small
    - Work or volunteer in your field of interest

Notes:

_____

_____

_____

_____

_____

_____

_____

_____

_____

_____

_____

_____

_____

_____

_____

_____

Notes:

_____

_____

_____

_____

_____

_____

_____

_____

_____

_____

_____

_____

_____

_____

4. You're Hurt/Wounded; Now What?

Don't forget your mental health. If you need help, get it for PTSD, depression, marriage or family counseling – whatever you need, get it. Don't be embarrassed or afraid to seek help if you need it. Transitioning is a stressful time.—D.R., Col (ret), Intelligence Officer, USA

First and foremost, Thank You! Besides sacrificing your time and family time, you've also given it your all, physically and mentally. Day-to-day operations, training, deployments, and more training for more deployments have all taken a toll on you to the point that it's time for you to part ways with the military.

Donna: In my job as a clinical case manager, I see the struggles service members have coming to this realization. Often, they still want to give more; but the military is saying, "We've broken you enough. Thank you for your service; it's time to move on." Most service members aren't ready for this, and will most likely go through the grieving stages we discussed in Chapter 3. Know that this is okay! Allow yourself the time to go through this, so you can prepare for and embrace your next adventure.

If you've become medically disqualified and will go through the medical boarding process (or currently are), you can expect an average time of one year from start to final separation/retirement orders (barring further medical conditions or complications and/or appeals). During this time, your first priority is to get yourself as close to optimal health as possible. Now, this may not be the same level of health you enjoyed at the beginning of your military career. However, it's essential to optimize your health—not only for your overall well-being, but to allow you the time to start planning for what comes next.

Each service has its own set-up to medically care for those injured in the line of duty. The more complex the care, the more likely an integrated care team will be involved. These teams can be made up of a number of medical and non-medical professionals, providers, specialists, therapists (occupational, physical, or mental), and clinical and non-clinical case managers. These teams ensure all aspects of care—medical, financial, and situational—are addressed, and all team members are aware of all needs. The clinical case manager is usually the pivotal player in a care team, because they ensure clear communication between the service member, family, and providers.

Usually, the nurses or licensed social workers are the ones determining the needs of the injured service members and bringing all the required "players" to the table. In other words, they develop the integrated care team. They assist you with pushing referrals through, finding appropriate treatments, providing education about your diagnosis, putting information into a language you can understand (versus all that Latin-based medical jargon), assist with developing an appropriate care plan for your medical conditions, help with your medical-care transition to the VA or civilian sector, and serve as your advocate and a great ear when you're frustrated or overwhelmed.

Most military medical facilities have case managers, and work within different programs. Typically, the more complex the care requirements are, the higher the odds you'll be automatically assigned a clinical case manager. If you feel you need assistance managing your care, the best thing to do is ask your primary care provider if a clinical case manager is available to assist you.

The Air Force offers Airman Transition Units (AMTU) at various locations for active duty members who have been injured and meet

AMTU criteria. The largest one is located at JBSA Lackland Air Force Base in San Antonio, Texas. For those not eligible for a patient squadron, clinical case managers are available to assist with complex care. Reserve components often have the most difficult time with coordinated care. Air National Guard and Reserve units that are not co-located with an active duty facility struggle the most to navigate through military medical care.

The Air Force recognized this need, and developed the Air Reserve Component Case Management Division (ARC CMD to shorten that mouthful). Located at the Air Force Personnel Center (AFPC) at JBSA Randolph, also in San Antonio, its primary responsibility is to put eligible Guard and Reserve Airman who were injured on MPA, RPA or Title 32 orders back on orders to receive medical care, in an effort to return them to duty or process them through the Integrated Disability Evaluation System (IDES). They are also afforded a clinical case manager and care coordinator to assist them with medical care, TRICARE issues, and questions regarding line of duty and the IDES process. If you have questions regarding MEDCON, contact your medical point of contact (MEDPOC) at your base's medical unit. They're all versed in the MEDCON program.

The Army has an entire command, the Warrior Transition Command (www.wtc.army.mil), under which exists the Warrior Care and Transition Program (WCTP), dedicated to treating the soldier's specific medical/rehabilitation needs, along with assisting them with developing goals and providing resources to aid in their transition to civilian if they're unable to return to duty. The program encompasses 10 major elements:

Warrior Transition Unit (WTU)
Army Wounded Warrior Program (AW2)
Comprehensive Transition Plan (CTP)

Triad of Care
Interdisciplinary Team
Career and Education
Internships
Health and Recovery
Understanding IDES
Access to Soldier and Family Care Assistance (SFAC)

Various elements will be utilized by each soldier based on their particular needs. The Warrior Transition Units are located at major medical treatment facilities (MTFs) for those Army Active Duty and Reserve Components who will require six months or more of rehabilitative care and complex medical management.

The Navy also takes care of Seamen and Marines, through their Wounded Warrior Office. Wounded Seamen are transferred to the Anchor Program and, depending on the severity of the injury, they stay either in barracks or designated Wounded Warrior rooms in the hospitals.

Each branch of service developed a program to assist wounded service members and their family with needs that surround medical, financial and transitional situations. They often are part of a care team, such as the non-medical experts on internal and external resources for the SM and their family. Once enrolled, an advocate will be assigned to the wounded warrior. The Air Force has Non-Clinical Case Managers and Recovery Care Coordinators; the Army has AW2 advocates; the Navy has Regional Non-Medical Care Providers; and the Marines have Recovery Care Coordinators.

The programs are set up similarly—assisting, supporting and advocating for the enrolled military member, to include comprehensive recovery plan development, medical/physical evaluation board guidance, housing, financial aid, transportation needs, career and educational resources, respite care, TBI/PTS support services, transition assistance, coordination with government agencies (e.g. VA, Department of Labor, Social Security Administration), local resources and continuation on active duty/reserves (Army).

Air Force Wounded Warrior Program:
woundedwarrior.af.mil

Army Wounded Warrior Program (AW2):
www.wtc.army.mil (click on US Army Wounded Warrior Program)

Navy Safe Harbor:
http://safeharbor.navylive.dodlive.mil
(click on Sailors & Coast Guardsmen, then Enrollment)

Marines Wounded Warrior Regiment:
woundedwarriorregiment.org

The wisdom of getting your medical care in order cannot be stressed enough. If your records are meeting a Medical Evaluation Board (MEB) or the follow-on phase of the IDES, the Physical Evaluation Board (PEB), clear and accurate medical documentation is needed for a "smooth" process. But c'mon, let's be real: there's nothing smooth about it. You're going to need to be in the best health possible to handle the major life changes that will be occurring in the not-too-distant future. For some, the biggest life change may be the actual transition from military to civilian life. For others, including the Guard and Reserve members, it may mean finding a whole new career. Remember our earlier story of R.V.? He's currently going through the IDES for injuries he sustained after an RPG attack. He's a traditional

Guardsman (TAC-P) on the military side and works as a police officer as a civilian. His injuries are so extensive that he's unable to work in either career field. He must completely change career paths.

Medical appointments and the IDES process can be mentally and physically time-consuming. No matter what, it's important to keep good track of where you are in the process and what you'd like to do when you get out. Yes, you have more to consider than the service member who's separating with intact health. However, it doesn't mean you can't follow your dreams. Might you have to modify them? Maybe, but to completely throw them to the wayside...no way!

What about if you have PTSD and/or a TBI, you ask? Well, you're going to have to be aware of your mental processing, triggers, and responses. Talking to a mental healthcare provider about your plans and concerns about the future early on will assist in decreasing the anxiety of transition, as well as helping you determine the best environment for you to thrive. It's important to remember while you may be in maintenance mode with your PTSD right now, as different stressors arise (e.g. the IDES process, transitioning medical care, finding work, applying for school, etc.) it may trigger increased anxiety, decreased sleep, and start you on a downward spiral. One of us (Donna) has encouraged many service members to increase the frequency of their therapy when they begin to display signs of stress. It helps them keep focused and on track.

What if you're in a situation like R.V., the Guardsman discussed previously, and have to completely change career fields? Or what if you know you want to do something completely different, but are unsure what that is? Well, there are a ton of resources out there for you. Our best advice is to start getting a feel for them as early as you can. A great place to start is the Wounded Warrior Program for your specific branch of service (links itemized earlier in the chapter). The Non-Clinical Case Managers, Non-Medical Care Providers, Warrior

Advocates, and Recovery Care Coordinators are all there to assist you with your transition.

While you're kept in a medical hold status, there are opportunities for you to enhance your skills and gain new skills for future civilian employment. REALifelines, E2I, and OWF are Department of Labor and Department of Defense programs designed to assist you in garnering new skills for future civilian employment.

> **Recovery and Employment Assistance Lifelines (REALifelines)** (dol.gov/vets/programs/REAL-life/) is a partnership with the Department of Labor, Bethesda Naval Medical Center, and Walter Reed Army Medical Center. The program's mission is to ensure that wounded, ill, and injured service members who are unable to return to active duty receive training for a new career in the civilian sector.

> **Education and Employment Initiative (E2I)** (warriorcare.dodlive.mil/wounded-warrior-resources/e2i/) is a DoD program to identify the skills of recovering service members and match them with career and education opportunities, to assist them with transitioning to civilian life.

> **Operation Warfighter (OWF)** (warriorcare.dodlive.mil/wounded-warrior-resources/operation-warfighter/) is another DoD Federal internship program specific for recovering service members. E2I identifies skills and any skills gaps, and OWF provides the training, education, networking, and resume building to fill those gaps and prepare the service member for their civilian career.

Vocational Rehabilitation and Employment
(benefits.va.gov/vocrehab/index.asp) is a VA program that provides job training, skills coaching, resume building, and assistance with finding employment.

If you're completely unsure what to do and want to see what you're suited for, there are a couple of websites mentioned earlier in the book to assist you. Refer to Chapter 3, and check Chapter 12.

The Importance of Connecting

Whether you're a Wounded Warrior or not, connecting with other transitioning service members and veterans is an important aspect of transitioning, for multiple reasons.

Civilians don't get it. Most are thankful for the choice you made, and are happy to give you a handshake and a "Thank you for your service" comment. No matter how well-intentioned they may be, however, civilians haven't been in our shoes. They may not understand the love-hate relationship with deployments; the concept of uprooting your family and moving every 1-5 years is often elusive, as is the "get the mission done no matter what" mentality, or making fast friends with workmates/neighbors and adopting them as surrogate family.

It provides a network of other veterans for potential future work. A veteran understands why you had a six-month break in employment when you transitioned. A veteran understands the mental adjustment that occurs. A veteran can translate your skill set and see your value much more quickly and easily than a civilian with no prior military experience. Mike Durfee, veteran and owner of Grunts Move Junk, gets it. "There is a certain camaraderie that military guys have that other industries don't really understand. No matter what, you have to achieve the mission. There is no giving up. It has to be done, so you get it done." (See Mitch's whole story in Chapter 10). At the end of this book, you'll see a listing of veteran owned/operated businesses. It's a good place to start.

Networking with other veterans becomes an outlet or source of comfort during troubled times. Let's face it; good or bad, change is stressful. If you have financial/medical/family/transitioning issues, it becomes just that much more stressful. Enter vet buddies! Maybe they give advice to navigate a system you 're unfamiliar with, maybe they help with care for your family, or maybe they just provide a beer and an ear. Whatever it may be, just knowing that someone else has been there and understands what you're going though is sometimes enough to enable you to decompress and move on.

On the flip side, you may very well be the "ear and beer" to someone else feeling overwhelmed and confused. You may or may not know the answer, but you may be able to guide them in the right direction, offer a resource, or just give a word or two of wisdom to remind them they're not on an island by themselves. Sometimes what helps us the most is to reach out and help others.

Action Plan: Get Well

- Clinical Case Manager/Care Team
    - Work with them to optimize treatment
    - Assist with medical transition to civilian/VA care
- Wounded Warrior Programs/Safe Harbor
    - Start early discussing transition options
        - Education
        - Work
        - Family assistance
        - Financial assistance
- Medical Board
    - Keep close contact with your Physical Evaluation Board Liaison Officer (PEBLO)
- Connect with other veterans
    - Knowing others that understand can ease the stress

Notes:

Notes:

_____

_____

_____

_____

_____

_____

_____

_____

_____

_____

_____

_____

_____

_____

5. Your Health: Physical, Mental, and Financial

Early to bed and early to rise, makes a man healthy, wealthy, and wise. — Benjamin Franklin

Just because you may not be a Wounded Warrior doesn't mean you shouldn't make or keep your health a priority. No one realizes how precious health is until they begin to lose it. You can bet that anyone who has ever suffered a decline in their health will agree. A life filled with medical appointments, medications, and more medical appointments isn't a life anyone wants to maintain for long. Much like any other area in your life that becomes disorganized, getting the pertinent areas optimized will be one less thing that causes your stress level to rise. Oh—and stress alone can damage your health. See the potential for the toilet bowl effect? One thing gets out of control and it can domino to other areas, causing them all to start spiraling down. In the same fashion, being proactive and getting control of ugly situations can cause dramatic improvements in your life.

It's important to be ready for the events to come. We can't emphasize enough how important it is to be as prepared as possible mentally, physically and financially. Consider this a "foot stomp" on the transition test.

Whether we like it or not, we're all military assets, and are required to keep in shape for our in-garrison and deployed jobs. Most veterans will agree that the best physical shape they were in was in the military. Although that may be true, it doesn't have to be. Don't let job requirements or the "scare" of the PT test be your only motivator to stay in shape. Grow a beard, get a tattoo in an obvious place, dye your hair purple, but don't grow a gut just because you can. You gave a lot to the military, and now it's time to go on to your next adventure in the best health possible.

Exercise

Don't stop being physically active! Exercise may be the best antidepressant for you. Nothing beats doing PT to not only keep fit, but to improve your attitude. It costs nothing, it can be varied by the day, and it can be done just anywhere, anytime, or in any form.

Remember Newton's Law of Motion: an object at rest tends to remain at rest, and an object in motion tends to remain in motion. If you stop, it'll be a lot harder to get back into motion, especially as you age. Keep using it, or risk losing it. While you may no longer need to be at peak physical condition so you can take on an enemy in a combat zone, do ensure that you keep up your PT so the stress from the many changes coming your way will be lessened.

If your favorite pastime is a gym workout, staying in shape probably won't be an issue. However, most people hate workouts. If you're one of them, we'll let you in on a secret: you don't have to be a gym rat to stay in shape. The key is to find an activity you enjoy and do it consistently. Just for clarification, consistently (according to the most current Physical Activity Guidelines)[19] means at least 150 minutes of moderately intense aerobic activity each week. That works out to a minimum of 30 minutes a day, five days a week. Anything above that, including muscle strengthening, is an additional benefit. If you're recovering from an illness or injury or just getting back to exercise, take

---

[19] health.gov; See *Physical Activity Guidelines* and the left hand menu *Adults*.

it slow. Start with whatever you can do: five minutes, 10 minutes, it doesn't matter. Just start moving.

So find things you like to do, or try a new activity like joining a running group, taking up yoga, swimming, biking, hiking, roller blading, martial arts, horseback riding or just walking the dog a couple miles every day. The list is endless. One person I know just picked up roller derby, and found that she absolutely loves the sport.

And again, it doesn't have to be done all at once. Intense ten minute spurts 3-4 times a day work, too. Run around the soccer field while your child is at soccer practice. Do push-ups, squats, and stair sprints in the morning, noon, or evening (or all three). Park your car further from the store, take the stairs at work, get a standing desk, use an exercise ball as a chair… it adds up in the end.

Donna: As a busy working mom of two very active kids, with a husband who is equally busy, I had to learn how to tuck PT into my day. I am that gym rat. I'd happily work out for an hour and a half every morning. However, I don't have that luxury. Instead, I get a 30-45-minute workout most weekday mornings before work, and then stay active with the kids after school and on the weekends. If I can't make a workout in the morning, I'll try to get in 15-20 minutes of yoga before heading out the door, or take my oldest out for a walk/jog. And if all else fails, a round of burpees gets the heart rate up and works the whole body in a short amount of time.

Whatever, you say? Well, here are a few stats[20] to motivate you.

---

[20] http://health.gov/dietaryguidelines/2015/guidelines/chapter-2/current-eating-patterns-in-the-united-states/#callout-changing-patterns.

- According to the 2015-2020 Dietary Guidelines, "Only 20 percent of adults meet the Physical Activity Guidelines for aerobic and muscle-strengthening activity."
- Of that 20 percent, males make up 24% and women 17%. Even more disturbing, 30% of adults report no leisure-time physical activity, even though there's solid evidence that as little as 10 minutes of physical activity daily can have noticeable benefits.
- People with lower income and education levels have lower rates of physical activity.
- Less-active occupations contribute to less physical activity associated with home, work, and transportation.

While getting up and moving are critical for overall health (we can't foot stomp/shout/bold type/yodel that enough), you won't get far if you don't have the proper fuel.

Eat Healthy

Between crazy hours, military schooling, training, TDYs, and deployment, maintaining a healthy diet can be a serious challenge. Everyone knows two places on deployment: the DFAC (chow hall) and the gym. The soldier's mission, combined with the frequency which they choose to visit each of them, seems to be directly proportional to how the uniform fits. Military food choices tend to be high in calories to sustain service members through the long hours they're required to work. However, it may not be very nutritious overall (ice cream bar, anyone?).

Once we get back home, the calorie requirement drops significantly, but our taste for the empty calories does not. As the saying goes, you are what you eat. No truer words have been spoken.

Your body is an engine that requires food to provide you with energy and resources to keep it running smoothly and in top condition. This means less processed foods and more natural foods. While eating a slice of pizza once a week won't kill you, eating half a pie a couple of times a week will take a long-term toll on your body.

Donna: When my children were toddlers, they were like many children, turning up their noses at anything they were wary of. The advice I received from family and friends was to keep introducing those foods over and over to influence their food preferences as they got older. Guess what? They were spot on. Both my kids eat salads, fresh fruits, veggies (with a big preference for raw... but hey, baby steps) and are self-regulating when it comes to sugar. If it works for children, then the same must be true for adults, right? Research says yes!

Kevin: I took one of the first EMT (Emergency Medical Technician) courses in 1979. The doctor that taught the course and the nurse that assisted discussed eating healthy. I asked after class one night how much salt should I use on my food? The doctor said there was enough salt in fresh vegetables and fruits to satisfy a body's needs for salt. Well, I decided to cut out all salt at my meals. Initially I thought my food tasted bland, but over time I began to taste the salt already in the meals I ate and then food began to taste salty. The same thing happened with switching from processed food to fresh fruits and vegetables and having home-cooked meals. Things started to taste different eating out after months of making meals at home with fresh ingredients. What a difference making smart choices makes in our lives!

A 2001 article review found that "processes such as mere exposure, Pavlovian conditioning, and social learning shape the relationships between these factors: food liking and eating behavior."[21] The more often a food is tried, the better it is liked. So keep on trying; you may just surprise yourself. Another interesting bit of information they found was some food dislikes may have less to do with the actual taste, but to a condition attached to that food (Pavlovian conditioning).[22] For example, suppose a person eats a particular food and subsequently gets sick. Maybe it was food poisoning, or maybe it was just a coincidence. No matter; now the person has an aversion to that food, because they remember getting sick after eating the food.

Donna: This happened to me when I was moving to Germany for my next assignment. I came down with a cold and took Cold and Flu Alka-Seltzer in 7-Up. It tasted horrible! It took me four years before I could stomach the taste of 7-Up or anything that was close in flavor.

So: if you don't like a particular food, ask yourself why. It might be because of what happened versus the taste of it. Bottom line, you can influence your food preferences. So although you drool every time you see a commercial for deep dish pizza, you can change your tastes by changing your food selection. If your choices for food are greasy and processed, you'll start developing a taste for greasy, processed food. Fresh fruit and vegetables will have little flavor to you, because your taste buds have become accustomed to food heavily laden with salt and sugar.

If you stop eating the greasy processed food and replace it with whole foods, such as fruits and vegetables, the food will start out tasting bland. Over time, however, your taste buds will readjust and

---

[21] Baeyens & Van den Bergh, p. 443.
[22] *Ibid*, p. 447.

become more sensitive to the flavors of unprocessed food. Once you adjust to it, a greasy burger will most likely not taste as good as it did before you adjusted your eating habits (nor will you feel very good afterward).

How people handle change is very individualized. The first thing to recognize is how you react to change. If you're an all-or-none person, then clean out that refrigerator of all the processed crap and fill 'er up with whole foods. If the thought of parting with your Wonder Bread causes you to hyperventilate, then take it slow. One change at a time.

Once you've mastered one change, go on to the next. Developing permanent healthy eating habits is not an overnight process. If it were, then everyone would be doing it. It's a process that takes slow, consistent change. If you tend to adjust to change slowly, then don't overwhelm yourself by making too many changes at once. However, do be adventurous. If you despise potatoes, maybe you'll love sweet potatoes. Not a fan of apples and oranges? Try some of the more exotic fruits: persimmons, jicama, mango, or papaya. Spinach not your game? Try kale. Or mix it all up in a crazy smoothie. Believe it or not, kale and spinach may turn a smoothie green, but they don't contribute much to the flavor.

Bottom line: you need to eat well as part of your overall well-being. There's no need to go on a strict dairy/wheat/soy/gluten/carb/meat-free diet. Just clean it up a bit and eat healthier. If you can't navigate to the fruit and vegetable section in your grocery store, but know the name of the fast food cashier's children... yeah, it's time to clean up the diet a bit. In most cases, "buy the outer edges" or along the walls of a grocery store, because that is where you'll find the less-processed foods. Shopping the inside means more processed food. Another option is to get outside, find your local farmer's market, or take the kids on a field trip to pick their favorite fruits.

Think Healthy

Not only do a healthy diet and regular exercise prevent that post military gut, but they're proven to be great for the mind, too. Talk about a double-bang for your buck! There's tons of research regarding the mental health benefits of exercise, for example. Whether it's depression, anxiety, insomnia, or stress, regular exercise can play an integral part of mood elevation and boosting your self-esteem.

The hormone cortisol is released when you undergo an increase in stress, good or bad. When bad stress levels rise, the mind and body are at a higher risk of depression and mental illness, as well as lower life expectancy. When the body can't lower cortisol levels, it responds in all kinds of funky ways... with cravings for carbohydrate-rich foods, weight gain, difficulty losing weight, increased blood pressure, increased cholesterol, increased risk of heart disease, lower immunity, etc., etc.[23] At the end of the day, the mind and body are intertwined, needing each other to improve, optimize and maintain your overall physical and mental well-being. When you feel good, you look good; and when you look good, you feel good... simple as that.

Donna: When I worked as a personal trainer, most people told me they felt better and thought they looked better way before they ever lost a pound.

The hardest part for most service members is admitting they're under stress at all. We're conditioned to "suck it up" and deal with whatever is thrown at us. Who hasn't heard the phrase "adapt and overcome"? However, once the stress level gets too high, it becomes

---

[23] mayoclinic.org/healthy-lifestyle/stress-management/in-depth/HLV-20049495).

more and more difficult to overcome. It may sound crazy, but transitioning out of the military may prove to be more stressful than being shot at, for the simple reason that the unknown (*what am I going to do as a civilian?*) is scarier than the known (*still in the military, and the risk of being attacked comes with the job*).

Kevin: When I was in USAF ROTC in college in the early 1980s, I had a Psychology professor who knew that I would be entering the Air Force after college graduation. He gave me a cassette tape of a recording of a briefing by Major (Dr.) William E. Mayer regarding the treatment of the American Korean POWs. I was shocked at what the military learned from returning Korean POWs, and took that information with me when I entered the service. Fast forward to 2004, when I established a reading program habit where I learned in the USAF to read a book a month and picked up the book *How Full is your Bucket?* by Tom Rath and Donald O. Clifton. Reading the first chapter on the first page, I sat straight up with my full attention devoted to what I was reading. I was reading EXACTLY what I had heard on the cassette tape about 25 years earlier. Long story short, it stated, "despite relatively minimal physical torture…the overall death rate of North Korean POW camps [was] an incredible 38 percent—the highest POW death rate in U.S. military history. Mayer had discovered a new disease in the POW camps—extreme hopelessness brought on by relentless negativity, the soldiers called this attitude 'give up-itis'." Out of this Korean War experience came our "Code of United States Fighting Force," or "Code of Conduct." This book outlines major steps on how to never get to "give up-itis."

One of the best pieces of advice I ever received regarding stress, whether PTSD or just the stress of dealing with change, is to write out what you've been through or are going through. Get it ALL out of your head and onto paper, including feelings, sights, sounds, smells, and tastes. Let it pour out of your without worrying about how it looks or sounds, or that someone else might read it. Just as physical exercise can get you more focused, writing things out gives a "voice" to your experiences or whatever you're going through now, via the outlet of paper or the computer. The act of writing itself leads to strong physical and mental health benefits.[24]

When you write things down, you get everything out—thoughts, feelings, and experiences—and then you eventually detach your emotions from the events, because you can take a step back and take a good look at things "from afar," given what you've dealt with and need to deal with next. Now you can be objective with yourself and others about what you went through. You can find parts you might need to take responsibility for, but in some cases, you'll find you take ownership for things for which you're not actually responsible.

Sleep Health

Another important part of good mental health is sleep. Judith Hansen, MA, LPCC, and owner of Power for Living, gives tips on how to develop good sleep hygiene:

It's common knowledge that sleep is needed for overall health—mental, physical and emotional. What many people may not realize is just how important it is. And for those who are regularly lacking sleep, it may be difficult to figure out how to reverse it. Sleep seems to be the first thing neglected when you embark on a new venture, a transition from one way of life to another, or feel overwhelmed. I get it. I've been there, and know how easy sleep can take a backseat to life's demands (kids, spouse, work, moving, and changing jobs). When I discuss sleep

---

[24] mic.com; See *Science Shows Something Surprising About People Who Love to Write.*

disruption with my clients, I find it most helpful to approach the problem like a detective: what are their bedtime routines? Do they watch violent or stressful TV or shows or news before sleeping? Is the bedroom quiet, dark and peaceful while they try to sleep? Do they routinely drink alcohol before retiring? Are they taking any medication?

Let's look at each of these potential problems in more detail. Perhaps this section will reinforce, reenergize, and validate your conviction that sleep is essential, especially when it has been an area of neglect. I hope this will give you permission to lie down and rest. I also hope the following tips will get you started on improving your sleep habits.[25]

1. **Establish a routine.** A consistent sleep schedule and bedtime are habits critical to a good night's sleep. For example, pick a regular time to retire (whenever possible), listen to soft music, read a book, take a warm bath, or find an activity that relaxes and signals your body that it's time to rest.

2. **Respect the bed.** Create a sacred space in your bedroom, removed from other pressures and distractions in your life. One thing I encourage my clients to do is to leave disagreements and fights for the next day, choosing to table them for the moment. There's nothing quite like a heated argument in the bedroom with your partner to weaken the association between bed and sleep! Finally, the TV, cell phone and computer have inherent stressors built into them. It's far too tempting to respond to that email or to a Facebook post, getting caught up in a drama or stressful show—all which sets

---

[25] http://www.healthline.com/health/sleep-disorders-prevention#Overview1).

you up for a poor night's sleep. I know this very well. Sometimes I need to remind myself to practice what I preach.

3. **Set the scene**. Check your room and compare it with these important details: Is your bed big enough, or are you bumping knees with your partner or half hanging off the bed? Is the temperature right? Do you often feel too hot or too cold? All of these are common causes of sleep disruption. Check for light and noise distractions, and invest in shades and sound machines or earplugs if needed.

4. **Mind what you drink.** Caffeinated beverages are the bane of a good night's sleep. They can disrupt sleep for hours. Whenever possible, don't consume coffee, tea, or other caffeinated beverages late in the afternoon or evening. Similarly, avoid alcohol. While alcohol helps you mellow out after a long day's work, it will also disrupt your REM sleep, the restorative stage of sleep. Finally, if you consume too much liquid, even water, this will cause you to wake up to use the bathroom. Limit your beverage intake before bed, and try to drink calming teas or warm milk, not water.

5. **Get up and try again.** If after fifteen minutes of lying in bed you still can't sleep, try this: get up and go through your routine again. Listen to soft music, read or take a warm bath. Avoid loud sounds, harsh lights or electronics, as this will make it more difficult for your body to relax and get back to sleep once in bed.

There are times when I don't follow my own advice, and lie in bed for a long time before finally falling asleep. Most often, it's because it seems like too much of an effort to get up. However, what does help is to focus on positive thoughts, to imagine myself in my favorite setting, or to hum a nice tune in my head. If I inadvertently slip into worry or anxiety, I refocus on the positive in my life, and remind myself that the next day is better to deal with problems. Then, oddly enough, the urgent "I must do this right now" and "I need to solve the world's problems" are seen for what they are: an overactive imagination in the middle of the night.

If you're in a place of rarely getting a good night's sleep and desire to change that, take baby steps. Pick one or two ideas/suggestions and begin to shift how you think about the habits you have, implementing them in your sleep routine. Give yourself grace for failure, and try again the next night. Acknowledge that you are on a path to learn, and that it takes time to change poor sleep habits.

Finally, we all need the support of those close to us when we know we need to make a change but struggle to do so on our own. If this is you, I would encourage you to enlist the help of your partner/friend/family member/roommate in getting to bed at a reasonable hour so you can get the seven to nine hours (yes, that many) of quality sleep your body needs. Sleep is so essential to mental health it deserves more than a passing mention. Consider how much your mental state is affected by lack of sleep, even when all is going smoothly in your life. Your symptoms will only worsen if you keep the candle burning at both ends.

Mental Health

If you suffer from anxiety, depression or an adjustment disorder (e.g., PTSD), you already know how it can rob you of a good night's sleep. As you begin to consider new ways to manage, reduce or be completely free of those symptoms, you may feel overwhelmed and think it a bit unrealistic that your negative mental state can be alleviated. This is especially true when in a depressive state. However, keep this in mind: lack of sleep can increase anxiety, depression and adjustment disorder symptoms. This inevitably leads to poorer sleep, which then further increases anxiety, depression and adjustment disorder symptoms. Vicious cycle, right? So, it is critical to know when to seek help to stop this maddening cycle. Sometimes a therapist can give you a new perspective and/or assist you in setting up an effective sleep routine; or perhaps a doctor can spot a health issue that interferes with your sleep. In any case, when you change even a few bedtime habits, it could be enough to shift the pendulum back to restful sleep, and give you a boost in your ability to deal with your mental health issues.

The tips and information below will give you the tools to manage/mitigate your anxiety and depression. The suggestions are not rocket science, but rather quite practical. Perhaps you will discover that reversing anxiety, depression or adjustment disorder is quicker and easier than anticipated. However, if your symptoms are not resolved in a reasonable amount of time, getting professional support is also critical.

Body. Chronic pain, prescription medication, alcohol, caffeine and poor diet are among the factors that impact how your body functions. This creates a cascade effect on your state of mind and how you deal with anxiety and depression. If you take medication, be sure you understand the side effects, including its interplay with alcohol or other medications. Check with your doctor, and eliminate the possibility that your prescription has an adverse effect on your sleep. If you avoid caffeine and alcohol before bedtime, it will have a positive effect on your sleep cycle. Caffeine can make you too wakeful to go to sleep, since it takes several hours for the stimulant to wear off. Alcohol can make you sleepy initially, but after several hours that effect will wear off, and but after several hours that effect will wear off and you will wake repeatedly the second half of the night.[26]

---

[26] pubs.niaaa.nih.gov See *Sleep, Sleepiness, and Alcohol Use*

Emotions. When you have a negative state of mind, it can certainly have a detrimental effect on a good night's sleep. Whether we watch violence on TV or have experienced/witnessed real life violence, our subconscious minds don't know the difference, and catalogue it as real. As a result, we may wake up in the middle of the night, worry about possible catastrophes, and create scenarios in which those we love and care about are harmed. Perhaps it stems from a horror movie or from a traumatic experience that actually happened. As a result, our minds replay these scenarios; sometimes once, sometimes night after night, in a hellish nightmare stuck on replay.

Your brain patterns its thoughts with the stimuli to which it is exposed. If it's chronically exposed to negative information (e.g. negative media, violent shows, real-life trauma) it will "see" negativity first in many situations. The same is true for chronic positive thoughts. The brain is taught to respond with positive thoughts. In instances of negativity, as soon as you recognize those negative thoughts and your anxiety ticks up a few notches, remind yourself that they're only thoughts, and intentionally turn your mind to positive images of kindness and love entering your life, with hope for a future that you envision. Soon, your fear center will calm down, and you can return to sleep.

However, this may not be enough for the service member who has experienced/witnessed war. Many of you have had front row seats to what most have never seen, and hopefully never will. Deployed service men/women are trained and conditioned to respond differently; to be hyper-vigilant, to have heightened situational awareness and to respond to threats (real or perceived) quicker than the average person. After months or years of this, it becomes difficult to shut that off. The more often you are deployed, the more difficult it becomes. The key here is awareness that you are responding differently to your family, friends, and in garrison and civilian surroundings. Don't be afraid to reach out for help. You may be trained not to break, but you *will* break if you don't get the proper help. Self-medicating (alcohol, drugs, eating disorders) is like giving antibiotics to an abscess. It just won't work. You need more. This means regularly seeing a therapist and mental health team until your symptoms are alleviated or mitigated. (*Molecules of Emotion: The Science Behind the Mind/Body Medicine* by Candace B. Pert, Ph.D. is an excellent resource for this).

Relational. A fight with a loved one, especially in the bedroom or just before bed, can have a very negative affect on both the relationship and a good night's sleep. My husband and I used to believe that it was bad (and even wrong) to go to bed angry. However, we didn't take into account how long it would take to resolve our differences. So there were times when we would stay up into the wee hours of the morning in order to "fix" the problem. Of course, no one is rational from lack of sleep in the middle of the night, and resolving a conflict in this manner is ludicrous and counterproductive. However, I wonder how often we think we should "fix" whatever problem we have by staying up late?

A general rule is if the argument will drag on past 9 PM, table it until the following day. I know that to go to bed angry with one another with unresolved issues isn't ideal either. However, if both parties can agree to let the argument rest, or to resolve the problem in the light of day, this will allow for both a better night's sleep and a more fruitful conflict resolution.

Spiritual. When you have a positive spiritual outlook—of self, or place and purpose in the world—it gives you meaning and significance, and will go a long way towards restful sleep. In other words, intentionally nurture a positive view of your place in the universe. This may mean you need to shut off the news for a while, or at least curtail the number of negative images and messages you receive daily. Sometimes we can get so caught up in the negativity that we forget that there are plenty of good, positive things happening right in front of us on a regular basis.

The following list[27] describes the benefits of a good night's sleep, along with the consequences of a poor night's sleep.

- **You're less accident-prone.** Your body demands sleep and will get it wherever and however it can. When it does not, it resorts to micro-sleep, where the brain goes off-line for up to thirty seconds while it tries to make up for lost sleep. The danger is that often, you don't know you've experienced a micro-sleep episode. While this may not be a problem when sitting at a desk (besides causing a loss of productivity), it becomes life threatening when you're driving. According to *The Atlantic*, "sleep deprivation…can physically and mentally harm people in myriad ways. Loss of sleep can cause hallucinations, psychosis and long-term memory impairment.[28]

- **You have greater brain function.** Greater brain function allows you to make the myriad of decisions necessary for a successful day. Without a good night's rest, you'll feel sluggish and be slower in reasoning, problem-solving, and concentration. These are all essential skills needed to make sound decisions as you prepare for and during your transition to the civilian world.[29]

- **It mitigates mental health issues**. If you struggle with depression and anxiety, look to lack of sleep as a large contributing factor. Mental health issues steal your

---

[27] webmd.com; See *10 Things to Hate About Sleep Loss.*

[28] theatlantic.com; See *How Sleep Deprivation Decays the Mind and Body.*

[29] http://www.webmd.com/sleep-disorders/excessive-sleepiness-10/10-results-sleep-loss.

productivity and joy of life, which leads to increased depression and anxiety. It's a vicious cycle that can be interrupted by a good night's sleep. However, seek professional help if good sleep habits aren't enough to manage your symptoms. There are many great tools available to help alleviate them.

- **It improves your memory.** As you transition, the details and stressors seem to multiply like rabbits. If you try to squeeze more tasks into the day and end up burning the midnight oil, you'll eventually suffer decreased focus, forget details, and lose track of important information. Prioritize what needs to be done and let go of things that aren't essential when sleep is on the line.

- **It's easier to maintain or lose weight**. A good night's sleep releases the proper hormonal functions. If you crave high fat, high-carbohydrate foods to get you through the day and manage stress, look to lack of sleep as a possible culprit. Proper sleep will help you maintain your weight and stay away from those pesky cravings. (http://www.webmd.com/sleep-disorders/excessive-sleepiness-10/10-results-sleep-loss?page=3).

- **It results in better overall health and fewer risk factors.** With a proper night's sleep, your body's immune system functions better, and you'll be able to fight off colds, flus, and infections. That fact alone can be a huge motivator to developing good sleep habits! Who needs the added stress of feeling awful when you have a full day's work that can't be avoided or put off?

A study by Harvard[30] underlined the importance of sleep on our health. Chronic lack of sleep can put you at risk for heart disease, high blood pressure, increased inflammation, obesity and diabetes, just to name a few. According to the study, "poor sleep leads to an increase in the production of cortisol, often referred to as the 'stress hormone.'" So simply not sleeping well enough reduces your ability to deal with stress normally.

As we consider all the positive benefits of a good night's sleep, we have to wonder: why it is so hard to just go to bed? There are many reasons, some of which are outside our control. However, when it's within our control, why do we sometimes procrastinate and stay up way past what's good for us? Perhaps the answer lies in believing that we'll miss out on something important while we sleep—like quiet or "me" time. We live in a stressful world with demands harping on us all the time, so it's natural and even expected that we crave a space where nothing is demanded of us: nighttime. And so, we stay up to savor it.

Just a thought.

Financial Health

We know that including Financial Health in this section might seem a bit odd, but money troubles can lead to a large amount of stress, which can in turn lead to insomnia, stress-eating, and lack of physical activity (because you're too tired from the lack of sleep and junk food binging). Therefore, we thought it important to touch on it again— even though this is a topic that most people, even in the civilian world, don't like to talk about.

We've already gone into the details on setting up a financial plan well before transition. However, financial health is critical. When

---

[30] healthysleep.med.harvard.edu See *Sleep and Disease Risk*

leaving the service, you may not have access to the type of support and resources the military offers. So where do you go for help? While there are non-profits out there that can help, there's no central place guiding you to their help, or helping you find the support systems the military is fond of having.

Of primary concern is you may be making great money, especially those of you in combat zones with the extra pay... but once you get out, you may have to take a cut in pay. So be prepared to cut back on expenses and spending now, even up to a year before you transition out.

Payday and paycheck timing. Your "1st" and "15th" military paydays and paychecks have been regular. In the civilian world, you may be paid every two weeks, but the dates may be different. If you're a contract worker for a temporary agency or you change jobs, your paycheck dates and days may change again. In other words, plan to have a cash reserve on hand to cover any "pay break" you may encounter when you're changing companies, organizations or adding new streams of income. You may not have the job protections you might expect as well. In "at will" states, when it comes to your job or work, "one day you're in, the next day you're out," as model Heidi Klum put it on "Project Runway." Plan and expect for marketplace changes, so you can keep your family finances afloat.

The lag in time before you get paid also means that when you change or start a new job, you may work for as long as two weeks or a month before you get paid. You may start on the 1st of one month, but you may not receive your pay for the first two weeks until the 1st of the next month. When you leave a company, you may not get your last paycheck as you start the new job; sometimes there are delays of one sort or another. That's also true of the first paycheck of the new job as you get "into their system" and things become regular. Don't leave yourself short of cash by failing to plan for these payday changes!

Also, take into account unexpected events that might take you out of work and leave you without a paycheck. It's easy to forget that unlike the financial continuity of the military, the civilian sector is quite different.

Donna: This was once made very apparent to me. I was bringing my kids to gymnastics and was at a stop sign where a gentleman was standing with a sign that had a picture of his two children. One child had leukemia and had just received a bone marrow transplant. Yep, I'm a parent and he caught my attention. I rolled down my window to donate to his selfless campaign and he noticed my uniform. We talked while we waited for the light to turn green and he told me he was prior Army; served two tours in Iraq; was injured in an IED attack and decided to get out because he couldn't go through another deployment. He was out of work to take care of his son and was raising money for a bed for his son that insurance would not cover. Just before the light turned he said part of him regrets getting out because he would still be getting a paycheck, and his son would be fully covered by insurance.

Bill Calendar. Create a bill calendar for all your monthly bills, but more importantly, include your quarterly and yearly bills and when they're due, too. This is to prevent any "unannounced bills" that become due that you missed.

Create a full year spreadsheet like the one below so you can see and plan your finances per your family's financial plan. Include all your bills, quarterly and yearly.

95

	Jan	Feb	Mar	Apr	May	Jun
Monthly						
House Payment	$1500	$1500	$1500	$1500	$1500	$1500
Food	$600	$600	$600	$600	$600	$600
Utilities	$150	$150	$150	$150	$150	$150
Gas	$100	$100	$100	$100	$100	$100
Quarterly						
Auto Ins	$300			$300		
Yearly						
Taxes				$2000		
Totals	$2650	$2350	$2350	$4650	$2350	$2350

The takeaway from this chapter is that your health and the health of your family are paramount. If you're too focused on how you're going to pay the next bill, how can you have time to worry about your health? It takes money to buy food and go to the doctor, so keeping physically fit will avoid the doctor, keep more money in your pocket, and keep your mind at ease for a good night sleep.

Action Plan: Maintain Your and Your Family's Health

Links to health and exercise sites:
http://health.gov/dietaryguidelines/2015
http://health.gov/paguidelines

- Stay Active
  - Try new activities.
  - Goal: 150 minutes of activity per week.
    - Break it up to fit it in.
    - Something is better than nothing.
- Eat Well
  - Cut down on processed foods.
  - Incorporate more fruits and veggies.
  - Start slow.
    - Make one change at a time.
- Mental Wellness
  - Keep stress down
    - Exercise.
    - Get restful REM sleep
    - Healthy Diet
  - Be proactive.
    - Have a game plan, but be flexible for the unexpected.
- Financial
  - Prepare a budget.
  - Save for transition.
  - Have a plan.

Notes:

_____

_____

_____

_____

_____

_____

_____

_____

_____

_____

_____

_____

_____

_____

Notes:

_____

_____

_____

_____

_____

_____

_____

_____

_____

_____

_____

_____

_____

_____

6. Doing What You Love

If passion drives you, let reason hold the reins. — Benjamin Franklin

So often, we're advised to do what we love, to follow only our passions in our drive to succeed. But if it were that easy, we'd all be professional golfers, fishermen, or couch potatoes. Just because you're passionate about something doesn't mean the money will follow, no more than thinking about something without investing action in it will acquire it for you. Franklin's quote (at the beginning of the chapter) means that you're to bring not only your enthusiasm, but your brain and your body to the quest to discover your talents and skills. In some cases, you may have to learn to love what helps you succeed, even the everyday, prosaic parts of maintaining a career or business.

In other words, don't be reckless in your pursuit of passion. Being passionate is awesome; it's the drive to accomplish what others may see as impossible. (Or in some cases, what others didn't even know was possible.) However, pursuing it with reckless abandon may not bring about the results you want—or any results at all, for that matter.

Some people might jokingly say they're passionate about wanting to taste-test beer all day, but in most cases, they probably lack the high-quality taste buds required to become a brewmaster. You might love doing something but are terrible doing it, or you can be great at something but dislike doing it. The true mark of finding your next adventure in life is the balance between where your natural talents meet your personal passions.

It all begins with finding your talents and skills first, passions second, then seriously studying what your market requires to earn a

101

living from your passions (unless you choose to volunteer your time). You don't start with how much money you want to make, and then find your talents. Your talents are those things you're exceptional at doing compared with others. Once you find that sweet-spot balance between your talents and passions and develop them, the likelihood of success grows exponentially.

However, let's back up a little first. Before we can utilize our talents and passion, we must understand what our purpose is. This is not to be confused with passion. Our purpose is bigger, more general. For example, one of us, Donna has always seen her purpose in life as helping people on a more direct level. As she has "matured" over the years, her purpose is more about connecting people. She's always been great at finding resources for someone. Here career has followed along this path of helping people. She is a military officer, a nurse (labor and delivery, flight nurse, and case manager) and educator (nurse preceptor, flight nurse instructor, and adjunct faculty), and now author. What's her passion? Well, it's actually more entrepreneurial and holistic in nature. Is it fully developed? Nope. But the ground work is laid. She's definitely utilizing her talents and skills (disciplined, multi-tasker, pretty good at writing, resource connector, good communicator) to do what she loves (health/wellness, building from the ground up) and fulfill her purpose (helping/connecting people).

How do you figure out your purpose? It's not like you get a fortune cookie with your purpose tucked inside (although that *would* make life easier). Donna was fortunate enough to be selected to present at a national conference about a year ago, and the guest speaker, Valorie Burton (bestselling author, speaker, and life coach), began talking about purpose. She used the word as an acronym, and it really resonated with us. We'd like to share it with you:

Picture the possibilities in your life

What is your vision?
What impact do you want to have on others?

Use your failures and mistakes as a learning tool.

Reach out
Reaching out to others.

Put things in perspective
What is in your control?
What is not in your control?

Operate with Optimism (most of the time)
What might be a more helpful way to look at this?

Serve
What can I give? vs What can I get?
When feeling helpless help someone.

Enjoy the journey

Isn't that what we were all put on this earth to do... to enjoy it? What better way to do this than to fulfill our purposes by using our talents/skills to unleash our passion? If we love what we do, how much work is it, really?

Growth versus fixed mindset

In Dr. Carol Dweck's book *Mindset*, she describes how having a *growth mindset* versus a *fixed mindset* can make all the difference between enjoyable success and not-so-enjoyable success, or even failure, in your career and life. As a psychology researcher, she became obsessed with how people coped, or didn't, with failures. While her initial focus was on the ease or difficulty with which children tackled putting together their puzzles, she was unexpectedly surprised that the difficulty or ease of the puzzle was not their issue.

Some children loved failure!

Her initial thought was, *what's wrong with them?* It wasn't the typical nature-versus-nurture (genes versus environment) issue; it was more than that. They didn't believe they were failing. They were learning! Rather than seeing their abilities, personalities, IQ, or talents as set in stone as a fixed mindset would have, doing the puzzle was the baseline to start from; and with effort, sometimes much effort, sweat, and even some tears, they could get better at it. They could get better at whatever they were pursuing.

For a person with *fixed mindset,* each encounter of a new event or task "creates an urgency to prove yourself over and over" and continually seek to validate who you are.[31] A fixed mindset also has negative self-talk in which the individual repeatedly tells himself or herself what a failure or loser they are. In Dweck's words, "they see what happened as a direct measure of their competence and worth."[32]

A *growth mindset* starts with what you're dealt as the jumping-off point of your development. Your basic qualities as an individual can be cultivated through your efforts, your strategies, and help from others.

Both mindsets show up in children and progress throughout one's lifetime into adulthood. Fixed mindsets occur even at high levels of performance such as in a company like Enron, tennis great John McEnroe, or CEOs Lee Iacocca of Chrysler fame or Albert Dunlap of Scott Paper fame. It's a *me me me* and a "need to be proven" mindset.

---

[31] *Mindset,* by Carol Dweck, p. 6
[32] *Ibid*, p. 8

They cared more about themselves than for the little guy. In other words, their words and actions came from "you're a genius" or a fixed mindset. Growth mindset examples such as GE's CEO Jack Welch, IBM's Lou Gerstner, or XEROX's CEO Anne Mucahy all started as growth-minded leaders that had a "belief in human potential and development."[33] It's a *we we we* and a "need to develop" mindset.

While most individuals misrepresent and inflate their abilities, those with fixed mindsets "accounted for all the inaccuracy" of individuals that were overestimating their abilities while those with growth mindsets were the most accurate. Why? Because having an accurate assessment of your abilities means knowing where you are and having room to grow and develop. The contrast is that any failures have been transformed from an *initiative* by those with a growth mindset (I failed) to an *identity* (I am a failure) with a fixed mindset.

So, do you have a fixed or growth mindset? If you determine you had a fixed mindset, no worries; it's just an area for improvement. As Dweck points out, "Effort is what ignites that ability and turns it into accomplishment."[34] And if you determine you have a growth mindset, congratulations! The world is your learning playground, and numerous adventures await.

Now that we have found your purpose and growth mindset, let's get into talents and passion.

Talents first, passions second

Among the most-watched TED talks are those by Sir Ken Robinson, titled *Changing Education Paradigms* and *How to Escape Education's Death Valley*. Any of Robinson's TED talks are worth watching, but the themes he discusses in these two talks resonate with

---

[33] *Ibid*, pp. 111-125.
[34] *Ibid,* pp. 41.

most of us in that we, as a society, need to cultivate creativity and acknowledge multiple types of intelligence. When presented with the statement, "At work, I have the opportunity to do what I do best every day," only one-third of workers responded with "strongly agree."[35]

Talents. *Talents* are natural abilities, innate and inalienable, that you inherit from your parents, and that you must develop to maximize.[36] These are your high-performance skill sets, like having a great singing voice. *Skills* are learned abilities, your lesser aptitudes, and are your medium-performance skill sets. While we all have both high-performance talents and medium-performance skills, developing and applying the combination of all of them can become a way for you to earn a nice living, or enjoy yourself by volunteering to do something you love. Everyone has a variety of skills sets that makes them unique. But exactly how unique are we?

Mel Robbins, a life coach, author, and CNN commentator, once noted in a TED talk that scientists have calculated the odds of you being born with your specific DNA at the specific time you were born to be about one in 400 hundred trillion.[37] That means you're VERY unique! Given your knowledge, skills, ideas, and motivations, you can change your part of the world.

If talents are what you were born with, then where do your passions come in? Here's a story that gives a good idea of what we're talking about.

Kevin: I was in the final stages of writing my first book, *How to Start a Business: Mac Version,* and I attended a book conference where Tama Kieves was one of the keynote speakers. She spoke of growing up, and writes about her life:

---

[35] *Ibid,* p. 2.
[36] See the book *Strength Finder 2.0* by Tom Rath and take the test.
[37] *How to Stop Screwing Yourself Over,* by Mel Robbins at TEDxSF.

I had always, always, *wanted to write. But I signed up for law school because encouraging, well-meaning people told me it would be more practical than starving as a novelist or journalist or we-won't-even-discuss-it poet. And I believed them because they drove nice cars and seemed to have a plan. ... So much for reason and practical plans. In other words, I chose this career out of fear, with the strange conviction that somehow if I worked in opposite to the voice in my heart, I would find security and fulfillment. ... Stifling my passion, I'd hoped for strength and satisfaction."[38]*

Kieves finally left one of Denver's largest elite corporate law firms to write, and eventually became a bestselling author. Today she helps others discover and soar in their life's work.

As you can see from Kieves's story, she was able to drive herself to perform at a high level, graduating from Harvard Law, but she was not passionate about using her talents in her current job, nor was she happy.

Not. At. All.

Why else would she leave? Just because you *can* do something, and can be very good at it, does not mean you *should* be doing it for a living. That's where passion comes in.

Passions. When it comes to passion, in reality, once you find what your many talents are, it is *who* and the numbers of people you serve that either make you money or not. Henry Ford said, "A business absolutely devoted to service will have only one worry about profits. They will be embarrassingly large."

For example, at any moment you can be inspired by an idea (e.g., a product or service). The passion for the idea grows and matures as

---

[38] *This Time I Dance!: Creating the Work You Love* by Tama Kieves, p. 15.

you start taking action to bring the idea to fruition. As you begin to market the matured idea, people start to love the product or service, and the validation continues to fuel the passion. Note a key word in this example: *action*. An idea is nothing more than an idea unless you take action, and to act, you need activation energy.

Activation energy is a term used in chemistry, as *"the energy level that reactant molecules must overcome before a reaction can occur."*[39] We're going to apply that to our topic of passion, and define it as the discipline to take action NOW! Activation energy is about being disciplined and forcing yourself to do things which you might be uncomfortable with at first. For example, marketing and promoting themselves or their business is often foreign and uncomfortable to many service members. However, the more you take on tasks that may be out of your comfort zone, the easier acting becomes, and the easier it becomes to act on future tasks

We mentioned earlier how positive feedback can fuel passion. On the other hand, don't shortchange negative feedback. It can be just as useful if it inspires us to do better.

If the inspiration is strong enough, then you might do research about a particular topic; master a new technique to elevate your skills; take classes; network, partner up with other skill sets, etc., all in an effort to develop the best product or service to offer to others. That passion to keep being the best self, developing the best product, building the best company, is validated when you offer it to others and they buy it/use it/share it. Validation continues to fuel your passion.

If you're changing careers, then your first goal should be finding what your main talents, skills, and abilities are (Refer to Chapter 3 on ways to assess your skills). Take actions with them and not only will you be much happier, but handling the curve balls that life throws is easier when you're doing what you love. Doing something that is truly

---

[39] chem.tamu.edu See *Kinetics: Activation Energy*

soul-sucking is tougher to battle, especially when faced with life's everyday stresses. Working your talents gives you that spark of energy, and you can do it all day long without breaking a sweat—versus doing something you have little talent for, which *saps* your energy and drains you. In other words, don't do soul-sucking work!

The three basic steps to finding a new mission or another adventure in life or a new career are:

1. **Find your talents.** Search out, dig up, or explore (or try new things you've never done before) to determine what all your talents are. This will also help you find out things that you find intolerable, like disliking the sight of blood or struggling with math. As you discover through your lifetime all your talents and passions, a natural inclination is to develop them because you're motivated by something that excites you. Doing something new for the fun of it is one thing; doing something as a new work or career will require the next step.

2. **Find your people or market.** As you begin further developing your talents and experience, moving from amateur through semi-professional to professional, do your research! Your market research will help hone in on your target audience. Hunt for others who need you to put your talents to work serving them.

3. **Serve your audience.** Once you have validated your product and service (i.e., found your target audience), provide the absolute best product and/or service possible to your customers.

That's it. (Okay, yes. we realize it's simpler said than done. But you got this!)

The three simple steps above encompass your need to grow, which means you need to get out of your comfort zone and *stretch* yourself. As Robbins stated regarding her Five Second rule, "If you don't take action within the first five seconds that you have the idea, you will kill the chance to do it."

Any action taken to improve your life is a step in the right direction. However, your best life is when you take action using your innate and inalienable talents/skills to fulfill your passion. When you're doing what you love, that energy spreads to those around you—customers, clients, colleagues, friends, family—either directly or indirectly. Some people enjoy directly impacting individuals, and others follow a more indirect approach. We've identified three overarching ways people impact others:

1. **Directly serving other people** (e.g. volunteers, social worker, teacher). This person wants to work directly with the person they are impacting. Their actions result in a more immediate validation and gratification.

2. **Serving people by developing/marketing a product** (e.g., computers, specialty foods, fuel efficient automobiles). This person wants to improve the lives of a population versus an individual person. A CEO of a company wants to put out the best product possible to better lives and increase profit margins (win-win).

3. **Excelling at their talents, in turn providing service to people** (e.g. professional athletes). This person is dedicated and passionate about improving their craft. The surfer will practice hours every day to be the best surfer. They may not be interested in serving any individual or population. However, if they want to make consistent income from the sport they need to not only win events, but gain fans and sponsorship.

None of them are right or wrong. Some people might even fall into more than one category (take the professional athlete who helps at-risk youths). However, talents (the things we are innately good at doing) and skills (the things we have developed and honed) influence how we serve other people.

Whether you have dreams in your new adventure of being a poster boy for your field, or someone who works behind the scenes within your circle of influence, you're out to find that perfect balance of talents, skills, and passions to live life to the fullest.

> *People who are unable to motivate themselves must be content with mediocrity, no matter how impressive their other talents. -- Andrew Carnegie*

Civilian to military, military to civilian

Prior to entering the service, you may not have had a full awareness of your talents or skills. There's a good chance you did not have a skills assessment done early on, or you may have had either a small testing or tryouts of what you were good at. When you decided to join the military, many of you (not all) most likely took the Armed Services Vocational Aptitude Battery (ASVAB). The test gave you a better idea where you had the most talent. Over the years, lots of training/memorable experiences occurred and skills were developed. Who you were never went away; but rather every moment, both civilian and military, was shaping and growing you.

Preparing for your new civilian career

In the service, the military provided you with your initial and follow-on training depending on the job that was needed, such as basic training, and then technical training in the Army's and Marine's Military Occupational Specialty (MOS), the Air Force Specialty Code (AFSC), and the Navy Enlisted Classification (NEC).

In the civilian world, and in most cases, you're now in charge of your own training, pursuing what you want to pursue since most businesses will not want to pay for you to learn. Larger companies may have the budgets to provide training, though with most smaller companies the burden shifts to the individual who wants to make themselves more marketable. It's always a good idea to improve your Personal Return on Investment (PROI), even if you must pay for it yourself.

In most cases, you'll have to talk with people in the industry to get a good feel for what it will take to do the job; or you can visit glassdoor.com, which provides insight reports and employees' choice winners about larger companies that might be of interest to you.

Whatever your choice, one thing is for certain: You're fully in the driver's seat of your career and your life now.

Civilian cultures differ from military culture

When it comes to transitioning from the military to civilian life, there will be changes that you need to expect. Here are some examples:

- **"Small stuff" is more important.** The "stuff" civilians worry about, versus your life dodging RPGs and bullets. Compare civilians complaining to restaurant staff about getting their cup of coffee "just right" versus service members yelling to your brother to keep their head down to keep them alive.

- **"At Will" Work.** In the civilian world, you could be laid off or fired at a moment's notice and never see it coming. In the military, it can happen, but for the most part, you're "in it for life" (unless you choose otherwise, of course).
- **Negotiating pay.** In the military, everyone knows what everyone else makes; not so in the civilian world. You must learn to negotiate what value you bring to your employer. Even then, you may outperform your colleagues by 10, 20, even 50 percent or more, but your organizational pay raise might be 4.5 percent increase while their raise is 4 percent.
- **"There I was" stories don't translate well.** When it comes to military stories and experiences, other veterans will get it; most civilians won't. Typically, the only way civilians get it is if they have long exposure to service members or veterans.
- **Civilian versus military culture.** Service members have their own "lingo," phrases and habits that are imbedded into the military culture, and civilians are no different. Some of the military's habits may seem robotic or to lack adaptability to civilians, while we consider ourselves trained, disciplined, and efficient. Or the civilian's habit of creativity or being adaptable is, to a military view, a lack of SOP (Standard Operating Procedures) or protocol.
- **Military leadership mentors and trains; civilians are mostly self-taught.** In the military, training and mentorship are cornerstones to successful development. In the civilian world, there is more of an attitude of "you're on your own," and you have to explore any new paths you choose for yourself. This is not only true for learning new skills, but in finding a mentor to assist you in developing your new career. The marketplace rules, and it's your new "enemy;" i.e. you need to keep an eye on the marketplace, constantly gathering market intelligence and

research, to keep current with your "training" and ability to "fight" in the marketplace "battlefield."

There are numerous differences in culture between the military and the marketplace, even between different companies. You may be shocked at what you may encounter. That is because cultures are different, but that's why it becomes even more imperative that you connect with fellow veterans already in the civilian world before and after leaving the service. They'll understand and guide you through this "minefield" of the cultural differences. (We'll get into more detail on connecting in Chapter 8).

From "Quiet Professional" to Selling Yourself

We've all heard the phrase about the Special Forces: that they're the "quiet professionals." And it's true; they tend not to want to talk about their successes nor about their missions, as do many military folk. Service members know who they are and what they've done and what they can accomplish. But whatever aspects about the military are true, going into the civilian workforce is about selling yourself to others about what you can do and what you can offer to an organization. The one thing that will set you apart from others is how well you transition from the "quiet professional" who may not want to discuss your exploits, to selling them on your talents so the person hiring you understands what you bring to the table.

Selling yourself is not necessarily just talking about your military missions and exploits, but rather what talents, skills, and experiences you have that a business, client, or customer needs to exploit to accomplish their "mission." It's about connecting with them so that you show that you bring value to their work. You have permission, right now, to tell others what you can do and how well you perform.

The key is to be able to tell them in the language civilians understand, so you have to put yourself in their shoes.

No doubt it will be awkward at first. But it will smooth out with practice and time. Here are some tips to help you market yourself without feeling like you're overdoing it.

1. **Be you.** It doesn't matter how many degrees you have or how many places you've traveled. Authenticity draws people in.

2. **Be interested in others.** Sometimes the best networking is learning and remembering unique aspects of another person's life. Finding out someone else's path/adventure can give you the insight to assist you on your journey.

3. **Develop elevator speeches.** Search out the right words and practice telling others in an elevator speech of 30 seconds or less what you can do for them.

4. **Practice reading body language/room environment.** This will allow you to better time questions and present information.

5. **Be interesting, not arrogant.** People like to know more about others with diverse backgrounds, not necessarily people who need to tell everyone their accomplishments.

6. **Be willing to tell people what you are looking for/interested in.** If you start talking to someone in your field of interest, mention your knowledge/interest/passion on the topic. Watch their response. If it is a positive response, offer a little more information. If not, leave it alone.

7. **Take advantage of opportunities.** Networking doesn't have to be a formal event. It can occur anywhere, at any time. (Think of meeting a potential date via a group of friends versus a speed dating event). When it presents itself, go for it!

8. **Have business cards on you, ready to share.** It doesn't have to be fancy, but it does need accurate contact information. At

the same time, if you want a higher chance of being remembered, a creative contact/business card could do just the trick.

9. **Keep practicing**. The more often you get yourself out there, the better the chance your talents and skills will be seen.

Every artist was first an amateur. Ralph Waldo Emerson

Assessing military talents, skills, and life experiences

We've discussed this earlier in the book. Whether you were a Navy SEAL and now want to be a farmer, or a USAF administrator who wants to become skydiving daredevil, of primary importance is that you harmoniously blend your talents, skills and life experiences with a game plan to pursue your passion. However, even though all that you've acquired will no doubt benefit you to some level, you still need to triage/categorize/prioritize these to best utilize them.

When you are transitioning, there are aspects of the military life that transfer with ease; other parts must be translated, and still others might need to be modified or even left behind. Find a mentor who will help you navigate these unwritten rules that lie just below the surface when dealing with others in the civilian world.

It's important for you to be aware of what skills and cultural beliefs you have developed in the military and know what to do with them when you transition. Here's a general breakdown of how to handle those things.

Keep and Honor

Dedication to duty, "no man left behind," a passion for our country and Constitution, and a host of other military habits are what makes you and our military great. Included with those are:

- Continue the mission.
- Arriving for meetings early.
- Being disciplined.
- Leadership/followership (as appropriate).
- Maintaining your appearance.
- Minding your language.
- Being polite with others (yes, including using "sir" or "ma'am").
- Maintaining your "military bearing" or the "power stance."

Self-discipline is by far the most important aspect of being in the military, and it remains crucial once you get out. The one caveat to discipline is for you to be able to change with the market, following where it's heading. Just as we changed from horses to cars for our transportation, so too must jobs and our work change over time.

Keep and Translate

Inevitably, you'll want to keep some of the habits the military taught you, such as "accomplish the mission" which is very similar to the civilian world goal of "taking care of the customer." But there will be some skills and habits that, while useful in the civilian world, you need to translate from "militaryese" into "civilianese" so they can understand what you did in the service.

Some of them are:

- **Acronyms** such as SpecOps (special operations), NATO (North Atlantic Treaty Organization), OPSEC (operations security), or MRE (Meals Ready to Eat).
- **Military terms or slang.** There's a small percentage of the civilian population that uses the phonetic alphabet shorthand (Alpha = "a" and Bravo = "b") or slang "Charlie Mike" (CM) for "continue the mission." While CM may not be used by you in the

civilian world, the concepts or ideas it carries may not go away, and needs a "keep and translate" approach or explanation in your new endeavor or chapter in your life. And we all know what "Charlie Foxtrot" (CF) means. It applies in the civilian world, too.

- **Phrases.** When it comes to jobs in the military, you'll undoubtedly use phrases like "putting rounds downrange." While this is a simple thought whether you're talking about a rifle, mortar, or tank round, it still takes skills to do the job. Translate that technical detailed phrase into an important trait in some career fields into "speed and accuracy when dealing with numbers."

Once you've taken the time to translate each of your skills into everyday language, identify your most sought-after ones and weave them into networking/marketing conversations with civilians when you're looking for a job or work.

Drop or Change

One of the hardest parts of leaving the service is the structured aspect of military. We have that structure for a reason; but in the civilian world, some of the habits we've acquired are not so clear cut. Here are some that need to change:

- **Automatically following orders.** Instantly following critical directions is of the essence in military missions, and any divergence can be potentially life threatening. In the civilian world, there is a higher degree of "pushing the envelope," questioning leaders about directions as to what is best, and redrawing boundaries at work. "Managing up," e.g. making your boss's job easier by anticipating what they want or need (NOT usurping any of their authority), is also important here. Civilians may want employees to be less structured and think outside the box more than the military culture; some more so than others, but it's a common trait that veterans need to learn about the civilian world. The expectation is toward achieving specific results, not a specific process to accomplish the results.

- **G.I. or Government Issued** is about having support from behind the lines to accomplish the mission. In most cases, in the civilian world a business department is more self-sustaining, with its own budgets and revenues, which means you may have to fend for yourself in your new job or career. While outsourcing will always be important, "handing off" something to someone else to fix a problem sometimes becomes more like "fix it yourself," except in cases like an IT department fixing your computer.

- **Respecting military service.** You may or may not get much respect from civilians; sometimes you'll get none, or even negative comments and behaviors from colleagues. Brace for it; don't expect it, but if it happens, be thankful. You did your military job so they could keep their freedom of speech, after all. Also, while the "there I was" story might have some relevance to what you encountered in the military, be open to the possibility that there may be other views to the situation that might require you to listen and learn.

- **Chain of command.** While in the military there is a distinct chain of command, and a less "informal" change of command; in the civilian world, it's not so hard and fast. Of primary concern is the issue of "sticking it out." When you sign up for the military, you're in it to win it and don't let others down in accomplishing the mission and getting things done. You "embrace the suck" and get it done. In the civilian world, you can be up and gone in a heartbeat, whether the decision is your boss's or your own. In the civilian world, you can change jobs like you change clothes.

Military-style tenacity may not as prevalent in the civilian world. This means there is a need for a "kinder and gentler" approach in how you treat everyone.

Depreciate and Lessen

Unless you search for a career in the civilian world like the one you had in the military, the thrills of a military career may not be so readily available. Here are some suggestions:

- **Managing expectations.** It should come as no surprise the military has one of the highest concentration of high-adrenaline jobs. Rangers, Navy Seals, Explosive Ordinance Disposal, JTACs, Green Berets, and Pararescuemen are just a few examples. It should also not be a surprise that there is a much more diluted population of high-adrenaline jobs on the civilian side. You may not find another "guns and gear" job with the related adrenaline rush, but you may find something with physical contact or exertion similar to what you had in the military. That means you might need to scale back your expectations some. If you are not satisfied, keep hunting! However, don't be dismissive if it's not 100% what you want. Sometimes starting with an opportunity that fills 60% of your wants can lead you to the next opportunity that fills 90% of what you want.

- **Higher income as a service member.** In some cases, military money and benefits are higher than in the civilian world doing the same job; in other cases, you'll get paid much more. It will be a little less of a shock if you delineate base pay versus benefits (housing, food, uniforms). The military provides us extra income (untaxed) to cover housing, food and uniforms (for enlisted only). Civilian employers, for the most part, do not provide this same benefit. So when you are comparing pay for a job, you have to take into consideration that it may be equivalent to your base pay, but not your pay with benefits. Government jobs are pretty stable and are slow to change compared with the marketplace. A civilian job can be here today and gone tomorrow.

- **Expecting respect.** We are fortunate to live in a time when most civilians highly respect us for what we did in the service. However, some civilians may not like or appreciate what a service member has done, or may be even antagonistic toward one's military service.

- **Wearing fatigues/BDUs/ACUs/etc.** Welcome to choices, diversity, and the ability to express yourself through your attire! Multiple variables will affect how you dress: job requirements, location, and personal likes or dislikes. Whether a suit and tie or a blouse and skirt are worn in the corporate world, or jeans and button-down shirt or even a T-Shirt in a startup, your dress code will vary. After work, for instance, if you were to go out on the town in Chicago or New York, you might dress "to the nines" with a suit and tie or black dress and pearl necklace; while in Denver, in most cases, it's business casual, nice jeans, and a nice button-down shirt, including the ladies.

Ignore or Bury

First and foremost: Yelling at others, directing or ordering others around! While bullets and RPGs may have been flying around those of you on the front line and would be normal in your mission's day-to-day habits, this will probably be significantly less so in most civilian occupations, depending on your career and the organization or company's culture.

What else to bury: bad language (such as using F-bombs in business meetings) and tough language can detract from your reputation no matter how good or tough you are.

Kevin: As was to told me, a former Marine came in and began demanding, belittling, and "beating his chest" toward a former officer's wife in their corporate civilian jobs, as if to pull rank on someone of lesser rank, expecting her to snap to when he told her what he wanted done. She understood her place and her job; he did not. He was later dressed down by someone with authority and he came back the next day profusely apologetic towards her and thereafter was much nicer. In the civilian world, there is a more informal hierarchy; do not ignore this. In addition, in the civilian world people do quit over stuff like this, while military members might go the distance when it comes to getting things done and being tough about a situation. Suggestion: *treat everyone, from the CEO down to the lowest worker in the company, with the same level of respect. Your reputation is at stake, and it can take longer to recover.*

Action Plan: Do What You Love

1. Determine your purpose
2. Find a new mission
   a. Find your talents
   b. Find your audience
   c. Serve your audience
3. Be aware and understand military versus civilian cultural differences.
4. Start practicing how to market yourself
5. Determine what skills, training, and beliefs you need to keep, translate, tone down, or dismiss all together.

Notes:

_____

_____

_____

_____

_____

_____

_____

_____

_____

_____

_____

_____

_____

_____

_____

Notes:

_____

_____

_____

_____

_____

_____

_____

_____

_____

_____

_____

_____

_____

_____

_____

_____

7. Connect with Your Community

Communication—the human connection—is the key to personal and career success.—Paul J. Meyer

It's a basic human function to connect with other people; we've each done it all our lives. We communicate with one another through our words, but actually *connecting* with others is different. Whether you give someone a hug, a high five, a fist-bump, or a shout-out, everyone is connecting. No matter how little or much, the need to connect is such a necessary action that a lack of it affects our health.

Research has proven that when babies aren't touched and held, they don't grow as fast as normal. The actual diagnosis is "failure to thrive." So biologically, it's a necessity to connect with others for growth. The same is true when it comes to connecting with others for *personal* growth; and it's personal growth that's really going to help you pursue your new mission in life. So how do we go about connecting?

First, understand that you're not alone in this transition; never have been, never will be. It's just a matter of taking the biggest step: reaching out. For some it comes natural to strike up a conversation with a stranger; for others, it might take a little more preparation and courage. No matter—once you take the first step to reach out and connect, the world becomes that much easier to access.

Never think or feel like you can't ask others for help, because help can come in many different forms: emotional, mental, financial, work opportunities; and from a variety of places – family, friends, individuals, groups, organizations, corporations. It could involve help with errands, a little cooking, walking the dog, mowing the yard, maybe even a chance to openly discuss and find differing viewpoints to improve your situation.

Fears keep us from asking for help: fear of being a burden, fear of admitting we need help, fear of owing a favor, fear of appearing weak, even fear of rejection. Suggestions:

- Ask for specific help; don't be vague.
- Change the fixed mindset that you're flawed at "getting it done" to view things from a growth mindset, where you're looking to grow and improve.
- Ask more than one individual who can help with your situation, and give and receive graciously.

Kevin: I have a friend who knows that I'm an author and asked me how he should approach someone who wrote a bestselling book about being in the Navy. He was a bit nervous about asking him for help. I told him, "He can say yes or he can say no, but you'll never know until you do ask him. He just might say yes. Ask, and if someone asks you, say yes, too."

Let's get a little more in-depth on connecting.

Connect with individuals

You are the average of the five people you spend the most time with.— Jim Rohn

Think about the five people you spend the most time with. Is it by choice or by circumstance? Now, compare their traits with yours. Notice any similarities?

Entrepreneurial and motivational speaker Jim Rohn's quote simply means that you're influenced by those you spend the most time with.

That influence can vary to include personality traits, financial habits, community involvement, parenting habits, or just overall life in general. This can have a positive or negative impact, depending on the influence. Needless to say, it is important to search out and surround yourself with those who personify the values and traits you would like to embody yourself. Keep in mind that you are as influential as you are influenced. Find your positive people, and you'll find that you positively influence others.

We're not saying anything you may not already know, but we feel it's very important to discuss the benefits of seeking out and connecting with others who relate to your military experiences and future plans. Connecting with those who have transitioned before you, and who understand the road you're on, is a great first step in moving forward to your next adventure. Utilizing other veterans' experiences or offers of help can be invaluable to you for multiple reasons.

- They offer insights and perspectives you may not have thought of, based on their own failure(s) and success(es).
- Their success proves that successful transition is doable.
- Their failures show that perseverance can overcome failure, and that you won't die if you do fail, because you try again and again until you succeed.
- Personal experience and wisdom (back to the whole "understanding the road you've been on" concept).
- Working through some of the various "minefields" of civilian life, such as legal issues, federal or state governmental programs, or confusing civilian cultures.
- Financial wisdom (you never know when you're mentioning your business idea to a potential customer or an investor).
- Their families can provide insight to you and your family.
- Their resources can run far and wide.

129

- They have friends in many industries, organizations and locations.
- Vets always have a friend of a friend.
- Vets are familiar with many government programs.
- If they don't know the answer, they probably know someone who does.

The longer you're in the military, the more "vet friends" you'll have. But it never hurts to practice those networking skills and meet more people. For instance:

- Attend informal "VetTogether" events with other veterans.
- Join groups such as veteran's, career, social media, industry, and most of all, your kids' hobby or sports groups.
- Get to know the friend of a friend.

All these can stimulate/multiply/brainstorm your talents, passion, and creativity in finding new approaches to your problems.

Donna: This book is living proof of the power of connecting with people. Kevin made a comment on a friend's Facebook page about the need of service members needing to find new missions when they transition out of the military, and it resonated with me. When I agreed with his comment, he reached out to me to talk more about it. The more we talked, the more I felt there was a need. I knew he was an author, and told him this topic should be his next book; two hours later, I became a co-author.

Kevin: When I got out of the service, I didn't want to have anything to do with the career that I had just put 13+ years of my life into, or any of the people involved. It wasn't until watching a TV show with

Navy SEAL Chris Kyle discussing getting out of the service and crashing (drinking, anger, grieving, etc.) that my ears and heart perked up. My wife turned to me and said I went through the same thing as he did. His comments resonated both with me and my wife. I had gone through it, but it wasn't until connecting with Donna and reading what we were writing that I came to realize what I had really experienced after leaving the service. I was able to put a name to it: I was grieving for my loss. After watching Chris Kyle, I decided then and there to extend my helping hand to any service member for any reason, to help them transition to civilian life. This was how Donna and I connected to write this book. Since we've begun writing, I have connected online with other veterans and have mentioned grieving in comment sections; some have responded that they, too, understand that they missed and grieved for the service.

As stated above, first and foremost, *we are human beings*, and we need to make connections with other human beings for our own personal growth. Having said as much, based on experiences from other veterans that have left the service, the very first thing you need to do *before you leave the service* is connect with other service members and veterans who are already in the civilian world in order to begin to create your new network, especially in the area you'll be living in.

Find a group of veterans where you move to when you separate. W.P., E6, 4 years Navy, 7 years USAR, Diver & Drill Sergeant

Be patient, but proactive in what you are seeking. Talk to others that have transitioned and stay positive. Maintain communication with your battle buddies, as those relationships are invaluable when coping with service issues that many civilians do not understand or comprehend. M.G.,

131

Lt Col, 3 years USAR, 22 years USAFR, Medical Service Corps Officer

Whether you had an ideal or less-than-ideal experience in the military, few civilians understand what veterans go through. Other veterans do. We don't leave anyone behind in a war or a conflict; nor do we fail in helping them find their new mission in life. The same standards apply for those who are leaving and who have left the military: we coach and mentor them so they can carry on with their new adventure for themselves and their families.

Another veteran will help you understand the stress of transition, the re-identification process of moving from military to job, and the importance of networking with both veterans and civilians. Less than five percent out of the over 320 million Americans have served in the armed services, but there are far more veterans in the civilian world than you can connect with. Don't overlook this valuable resource, as this connected companionship is sorely needed in the civilian sector.

There is nothing nicer than someone you can relate to. Connecting with individuals who have had similar experiences allows for a bond and connection that can be forever enduring. We connect on a variety of levels: the unit we were in, gender, race, religion, careers, values… the list goes on. It's not as important who you're connecting with, as it is that you start connecting and keep connecting. This is how a network is created, and this is how things will begin to happen.

Donna: I'll give you an example. Part of this book is comprised of interviews from other transitioning service members and veterans. I was talking to my best friend about the struggles of collecting interviews, and she was telling me about a veteran she knows who is starting his own business. Ironically, my best friend also has a degree in media and did a full interview on him (they live in Vermont and I'm

132

in Texas), based on the questions I supplied her. That led to an awesome success story you'll be reading in Chapter 12, and it, too, is filled with networking success.

You may be surprised to find that you have commonality with civilians in ways that may not have thought of. There are plenty of people who have had jobs that required frequent moves, time away from family, handling the loss of a close friend, similar upbringings, similar values, etc. That "I've been there and I know what you're going through" understanding can provide one strength during difficult times. You may find yourself the recipient, receiver, or maybe both. Any way you look at it, you will only benefit.

Kevin: Part of connecting with other individuals means more than connecting as a veteran. In some cases, it could be your new career, work, or new adventures outside of being a veteran. I started my own business and was hired by a friend who wanted me to help her mother, who was about my age, start her own business. She was an editor/writer and wanted to take her 80 articles of 750 words each and convert them into a book. I asked her daughter a few days later what she thought of my two-hour coaching/mentoring session and what her next steps should be. Her reply? "I have NEVER seen my mother SO excited in her life!" When I tell others what I do, the "successful suits" want to know how successful I am and what up-and-coming BIG companies I have helped; i.e. they're expecting familiar people and business names in the start-up or business community. When I tell that what I told you above, they disconnect and I'm dismissed with an attitude of, "Talk to me when you're really successful." Steve Jobs and Bill Gates never graduated from college, but started their own companies and became billionaires. It's not where you're from in your past or where you are right now; it's where you're heading into the future that matters! Your success or failures in your past do not define you or your future.

As with anything, change can be uncomfortable, and in some cases, downright scary or fearful. Having the support of people who have been through transition and can share experiences, resources, and tips is invaluable. The more you can adapt and change for the better, the better the chance of you breaking through to the next level.

A person with a new idea is a crank until the idea succeeds.—Mark Twain

Sometimes you have to prove yourself in the civilian world. Some people may be skeptical or dismissive. Civilians may not get you and your new mission in life. Expect it and prepare for it. As veterans, we should neither close the door nor burn the bridges to those civilians who may not understand us. Instead, see this as an opportunity to share and learn from each other.

On the other hand, connecting with other veterans should be like connecting with an extended family member or long-lost relative, no matter the branch, rank, age, or war or conflict. Connecting with veterans is easier for the simple (and obvious) fact that you have a commonality— whether that be the same service, unit, battalion, deployments, or just that you were both in the military. Those veterans who have gone on before you lead by example on how to navigate civilian life. All veterans, WWII to GWoT, are valuable sources of information. The older generations are great reminders of how far we've come, and the younger generations can provide transition experience. All of them have resources that could help you during your transition. So take the time, practice your networking skills, and see where it leads. Besides, your money may not be any good around them at the VFW post during "beer call."

A true friend unbosoms freely, advises justly, assists readily, adventures boldly, takes all patiently, defends courageously, and continues a friend unchangeably.—William Penn

Connect with organizations

There are literally thousands of organizations at the local, state, and national levels that are geared toward aiding the veteran. That is a staggering number! However, it's amazing how many transitioning service members and veterans don't know where to turn. We've done some of the research to get you started, and you'll see links throughout this book and in the Appendix that can help. Let Google be your friend, and do your own research. Yes, the volume of information can be overwhelming; yes, it may mean putting your pride/ego aside and saying, "I need help." No, it doesn't mean you're weak. What do you have to lose?

And who knows? It may lead you to another great reason for connecting with organizations: volunteering. There's nothing better for the soul than helping others. Whether it's giving your time for an event, a group, or an individual, it's time well-spent. Giving back to others can put life back into perspective. Those issues you have may seem trivial compared to those whom you help.

Volunteering is also a great way to find out if a field you're interested in is suited for you before you make too much of an investment in one direction. Be bold; some places that don't have volunteers may have simply never have thought of having one. So ask!

As we've said before: keep connecting. You never know what impact you will have, nor will you know the impact that others will make on you unless you take a chance and connect.

Here are just a few websites that provide help to veterans:

- **Veterans of Foreign Wars** (vfw.org)
- **USO** (uso.org)
- **Make The Connection** (maketheconnection.net) is an online resource designed to connect Veterans, their family members and friends, and other supporters with information, resources, and solutions to issues affecting their lives.
- **National Veterans Foundation** (nvf.org) helps veterans and their families who are enduring a crisis or who have a critical need for help.
- **Support Veterans and Active Duty Service Members** (charitynavigator.org) helps with charities that report their financial status and how effective they are. They give insights as to whether or not you want to pursue them for help.
- **American Veterans** (amvetsnsf.org). The AMVETS National Service Foundation provides veterans, donors, advocates, and volunteers the organization they require to ensure veterans and their dependents are provided counsel, and are represented before the Veterans Administration (VA) without charge every day.

When it comes to searching for help, while the list above and this book and its resources give you a basic outline of what you can find out there, things do change. Doing a Google search can find new and more current or up-to-date information and organizations; and be aware that some information may be conflicting. For instance, some organizations may claim 501(c)3 status on their website but are not registered with the IRS. They can still be helpful with your new adventure.

One of the worst things that can happen to a service member is their withdrawal after leaving the service, preventing them from connecting with others, especially other veterans.

Connect with your grassroots community

Kevin: What started as a LinkedIn connection, then a comment about transitioning veterans on a LinkedIn post, led to about an hour-long phone call with a lady discussing issues such as WWII veterans in assisted living having trouble getting appointments at the VA, veterans unaware of corporate programs that can provide them assistance and discounts, and veterans feeling abandoned and disconnected after leaving the service, and thus disengaging from others. The issue that came front and center after an hour: Community. The issue is that sometimes veterans can be less connected or disconnected within or with their local community than their civilian counterparts. Take the initiative. Be more proactive. Reach out to others to get connected within your community.

It's about you and your community, cooperating locally, together, for your community's betterment—and your own.

Once you have found work and a place to live, your next step is to expand your roots into your local community and become involved. To continue to serve.

You and your community are exactly what Leonard E. Read wrote about in his essay *I, Pencil: My Family Tree.*[40] It takes many individual and organizational resources working together to not only produce a simple pencil, but ultimately prosperity for all. Read's essay is also echoed by Brad Feld, of Tech Stars fame in Boulder, Colorado, in his book *Startup Communities.*[41] Whether it's the larger local community you

---

[40] econlib.org. See *I, Pencil: My Family Tree as told to Leonard E. Read*
[41] techstars.com.

live within, or the smaller veteran community, the main principle both Read and Feld share is that it's never about having a strategic plan when it comes to you and your community. It's not about wading in and through bureaucratic mud that stifles people's initiatives, but it *is* about everyone having good hearts wanting to produce a rising tide that lifts all boats within your community. But what is the one thing that makes it happen?

Community is about connections.

Veterans need to connect.

Veterans need to connect with their communities.

Veteran Connection

When you leave the service, you are an "entrepreneur" in the sense that you're a part of your community. There are major elements to having a vibrant and prosperous veteran community, and making a difference within your local community. They include:

- You need to connect to serve and develop trust-based interpersonal relationships.
- You need to build a collective network within the veteran and local community.
- You need to have long-term commitment to your work, home life, and local community.
- You need to be inclusive and open with your efforts by inviting other veterans, local businesses, and those that want to participate into your circle of influence in your endeavors.
- You need to be part of their grassroots community to have an impact on improving everyone's life.

Action Plan: Reconnecting

- Identify the values and traits important to you.
- Find people the embody those values and traits.
- Continue to connect with veterans throughout your transition.
- Connect with different generations of veterans for the broadest insight.
- Connect with organizations.
- Utilize available resources.
- Volunteer.

Notes:

_____

_____

_____

_____

_____

_____

_____

_____

_____

_____

_____

_____

_____

_____

Notes:

_____

_____

_____

_____

_____

_____

_____

_____

_____

_____

_____

_____

_____

_____

_____

_____

8. "Charlie Mike" in the Marketplace

Being busy does not always mean real work. The object of all work is production or accomplishment, and to either of these ends there must be forethought, system, planning, intelligence, and honest purpose, as well as perspiration. Seeming to do is not doing. —Thomas Edison

Charlie Mike is a book by Joe Klein that describes true stories of heroes who brought their service on the war front to their new adventure on the home front. "Charlie Mike" is also the radio communications phonetic alphabet slang for "continue the mission." Your mission to serve really *does* continue when you leave the service, it might take several tries to find the right fit in the marketplace. But don't let that slow or get you down.

Active and reserve duty service members have one primary mission: to defend our nation against all enemies, foreign or domestic, whether on land, sea, air, or in cyberspace. If you're not directly involved with the mission on the front line, then you're directly supporting those on the front line. When you hang up your uniform, you're now supporting the troops as a veteran and civilian taxpayer, but you can also continue to protect and serve by either going into the National Guard, law enforcement, or continue to serve with many of the organizations such as the Civil Air Patrol or a local ham radio organization.

Oftentimes, many veterans find they want to continue service-oriented work after leaving the military. The focus will pivot to serving your customers, whether it's being a coffee barista, an Emergency

Medical Technician, or an electrical engineer constructing the next version of the iPhone. While you switch your focus of all your talents and skills towards someone or something different, your end game is still service. Becoming a civilian, you'll search for your next adventure (work or volunteering) that helps or improves someone else's life—directly or indirectly.

When it comes to your life in the military, in most cases you were told what to do and when to do it. Now that you're leaving the military, you're in charge of your life. You've given your time and talent in the service of your country; now it's your time to take care of you and your family first, and then your community.

As we discussed earlier, the military training you acquired has skills that are readily transferable to the civilian world. It's just a matter of converting them into civilian terminology and concepts, so people understand what you can do for them.

Moving from military to civilian

Military and civilian thinking levels. The military and the civilian marketplace aren't that much different, but when you consider your talents and skill set and getting out of the service, they may use different words or terms. Below is an example showing how the military and civilian concept hierarchy can be parallel, albeit with different intended outcomes.

	Military	Civilian
Idea/Concept	Skunk Works	Research and Development
Top Level	Strategy	Business Ownership
Mid-Level	Mission	Project Management
Low Level	Tactics	Technician

A note for you budding entrepreneurs: According to Michael Gerber's book *The E-Myth Revisited,* most entrepreneurs fail because they're too focused on the low "technician" level, what they love to do and work at, and ignore the upper business owner and project-management thinking levels. ALL levels of thinking are important in getting the job done, and in keeping your revenue and income coming in.

Find a job, work, a new career, and an adventure

There are three words that describe what we ascribe: find a *job*, find your life's *work*, and live a *life*. First, finding a *job* means getting something that pays the bills and can be considered temporary on your career path. Working as a janitor or even working for specific organizations might not be your first choice of work, but at least you're employed and paying the bills. You also may find that the job you got may not be want you wanted or were sold as by the organization. No matter; learn the good, the bad, and the ugly from every encounter, as it applies to you finding a new career post- military.

Second, when you are looking for *work,* this means you want to find something that's more fulfilling and more aligned with what your talents are and what you love to do. How does this play out? If I came

145

up to you as employee and you were an employer and I said, "Hey, I'm looking for a job," what do you think your perception or reaction toward those words would be versus if I said, "I'm looking for work"? Inevitably, looking for work sounds more opportunistic, broader, negotiable, while looking for a job is just looking for a paycheck.

What employer would hire someone who was looking for a paycheck versus someone taking an active interest in providing value to their business and customers? Using the word "work" can also begin a negotiation process, where both a potential employees and employer each bring things to the table to provide value to each other.

Most businesses don't mind investing in their people, if they have the budget for it. It takes weeks, if not months, for an individual to get fully seated into a work routine and to become productive to a business. This can be costly for any company, but is especially true for smaller companies.

Start your own business as an entrepreneur

Leaving the service, you're starting a new mission: I call it *Operation Boots to Business,* or a different take, *Service to Startup.* Too often, educational establishments and government institutions offer content that might seem plausible for you to follow to start a business. But the intel from those "in the trenches" of startup and business industry (educational and governmental organizations) are not always up to speed with what a new veteran entrepreneur may need. In fact, their content is sometimes up to 5-7 years *behind* what the market is doing. While basic content like accounting or marketing may not change, changes do occur with critical needs like programming languages or eCommerce technologies.

Don't misunderstand; education is important, and so is learning. So, the question becomes: What's the quality of the content you learn, and from where do you learn it from in order to start a business? For example, while educational institutions might teach you the ins and outs of how to write and write well, they may not teach you how to write a book, design it, or how to market and sell your writings in the marketplace. They'll teach you the *craft of your business*—becoming a writer, doctor, lawyer, or a computer programmer—but they fail at teaching you the *business of your craft,* how to make money with your new skills and knowledge. Taking any and all business courses will provide a stronger business foundation for starting your own business than nothing at all, but even then, not all an education organization's content is worth the price you pay. Bottom line: Make sure you weigh your return on investment.

Definitions. An *entrepreneur* is someone who takes risks; someone who develops, shapes, and readies for market something that challenges the old guard and creates new and different value in the marketplace for companies, customers, and society. For most successful entrepreneurs, it's as much about adding to or changing the marketplace for the better as it is about the money. Money is still a motivator, but if it's the only motivator, you may run into motivational trouble. A *small business* as a rule is an already functioning business or franchise idea that's proven, has a fully developed infrastructure supplying it, may not grow beyond a certain level, looks to grow slowly and steadily, and is familiar to customers (a hair salon, a BBQ joint, a car wash). It's a smaller version of a large company. A *startup* is a newly established business that challenges the marketplace (mostly unproven, and in most cases with an oversized amount of risk (such as Uber, AirBNB, Facebook, etc.), is designed for *scale and sale* (has a potential exit strategy) which in most cases is unconstrained by geography, and has one or many founders. While both a *small business* and a *startup* are similar, the methodology of how both operate both internally and externally, scale, and funding are different.

147

A *solo entrepreneur* is someone who creates a single startup or business. A *serial entrepreneur* is someone who builds a successful startup and sells it and starts up another one; they sequentially start, build, and sell each of their businesses. A *parallel entrepreneur* creates and runs multiple startups or businesses at the same time.

When it comes to starting your own business, your hard-earned money and the time devoted to your new adventure does not need to be wasted. It is very important that you find the right content in the marketplace you need for the goals you have.

Potential. The 2007 U.S. Census Bureau's Survey of Business Owners[42] reported that:

- There were 2.45 million businesses with majority ownership by veterans.
- Veteran-owned firms represented 9 percent of all U.S. firms.
- Among veteran-owned employers, 78 percent had sales of $100,000 or more, while 38 percent had sales of $500,000 or more.
- More than half (53 percent) of veteran-owned employer firms had from one to four employees.
- Most businesses had only one owner, including 78.9 percent of veteran-owned firms, compared with 61.3 percent of all firms.

Watching TV shows such as *Shark Tank, Undercover Boss, How It's Made,* and *The Profit* have similar questions that are asked of every startup entrepreneur:

- What are your sales/revenue? If you're not making sales, you're not hustling or not listening to the market.

---

[42] See *Veteran-owned Businesses and their Owners—Data from the Census Bureau's Survey of Business Owners* at <u>sba.gov</u>

- Over what period do your sales occur? What is your growth rate: slow, fast, or "to the moon"?
- Are you profitable? If you're not taking an income, you may have expenses that are out of line with your business—and you're failing. Read the book *Profit First* by Mike Michalowicz to understand this issue better.

These three essential questions set the tone for the rest of their interview of any startup business. The follow-on questions are:

- What do you bring to the table?
- Why do you need our money?
- Is your product unique?
- How much debt/inventory do you have?
- What are your costs?

If you can't answer these questions in a positive way—if you're not showing business growth—you won't get their investment money. They also want to ensure you have skin in the game, so you had better be hustling for your own business, i.e. making sales, and not expect them to do your business for you. If it means you sell some of your unused stuff, take broken aluminum window frames and sell them for scrap to get the money so can buy a tool that helps you get your business moving, *that* is hustling.

Don't bring a backhoe to a job when garden trowel will do. When it comes to large organizations, such as the federal government, the military, and Fortune 500 companies, they have well-established and detailed processes in place, with specialists doing their assigned steps in these many-stepped processes, and in most cases, doing volume work with their one step.

Too often, people with experience in large organizations who intend to start their own businesses bring the same large-process mindset and toolset to their new business. Bring your good military disciplines and habits to your startup's problems, but don't bring a backhoe (a large, detailed process) to work in your garden when a garden trowel (a simple solution) is needed.

Kevin: For example, Adobe's InDesign is one of the "heavy weights" in creating books for publication. But I have used Apple's iWork Pages to write and create books, and have been able to produce two books with it—and it's free. Pay just enough to get the job done!

In the startup world, all content that discusses writing a *Business Plan (BP)*, a backhoe, is today taking a back seat in the startup business sequence to a new approach in which nearly all service members can achieve their dream job or work out of the gate quicker. It's called *Business Model Generation (BMG)*, a garden trowel. A BP is intended for investors, a BMG for customers.

Business Model Generation is for startups

When it comes to creating a startup, Business Model Generation (BMG, businessmodelgeneration.com) is the best approach today. BMG helps focus a startup's search for a business idea and model that is successful, then scales to grow their market. It's changing what was previously standard business advice: *write a business plan.*

The premise of BMG is this: *search for success, then scale for success.* Searching for success means finding a Minimum Viable Product (MVP). An MVP is a product with a minimum number of features or a production batch (five versus 50, 10 versus 100) large enough to validate your idea and begin selling to bring in revenue. The MVP approach is often less expensive than developing a "full-featured" product, which increases your costs and risks if the product fails to sell.

The concept of BMG entails getting your product or service into the marketplace, into your ideal customer's hands, to see what kind of market response you get—not only to get feedback, but also to see if you can make money with your idea. As the saying goes, if you can't or aren't selling your product to 10 customers, there's a high probability you won't sell it to 10,000.

Business Model Canvas (BMC)

Key Partners	Key Activities	Value Propositions	Customer Relationships	Customer Segments
	Key Resources		Channels	
Cost Structure			Revenue Streams	

BMG means you produce and sell your product or service, and from your higher margin profits you fund your business growth. In fact, one of the most successful real estate companies, Keller-Williams, has a best practice motto for spending and funding real estate business growth which applies equally across any startup business: "Lead with revenue!" If you're not making sales, resist any temptation to spend unnecessary money or go into debt to make your business grow (see the company 37Signals.com and find out how some companies grow organically, bootstrapped with sales and profits and no investors: 37signals.com/bootstrapped).

The focus behind BMG is to test, test, test, and test again your idea to see if you have an MVP. It's about having a *presentable* product for customers to buy, not a *perfect* product. Only when you begin to get more and regular customers that provide feedback to your product will you get opportunities to find ways of improving your business idea and model.

Skip working on and completing a BP to get you started; the BMG uses the Business Model Canvas (BMC) instead. The BMC outlines the necessary business infrastructure you'll need to become a business success. The BMG/BMC is to Special Operations, a light, quick small platoon that can respond and change with the situation, as a BP is to a Marine Battalion, a heavy mass of men and machine overrunning another large force.

While the BMC Table is a quick overview of the BMC and what you need to fill out and follow up on, you'll find more detailed information at the BMG website and in the book *Business Model Generation* about the BMC format.

Example: BMG versus BP. Using a BP approach is about you spending money and opening a bakery and then working to sell your breads, cakes, and candies to your customers. This older approach to opening a bakery means having monthly expenses of your or your family, friends', or investor's hard-earned money going out the door before you ever have any sales. Conversely, with the BMG process, you first find customers who are interested in your goods, make sales, and gain a following of fans and profit. After gaining a steady stream of sales and fans, then you find a local company that will provide you with shelf space so you can further test and grow the market. As you acquire more and more sales and success, you may branch out and get more local companies to carry your product. Only when you have small successes do you consider opening your own bakery. Apple sold its computers in third-party stores until it grew big enough to open its own Apple Retail stores, doing things its own and much better way.

It is highly recommended that you pursue the BMG approach initially, as this is intended to get you out the gate quicker regarding business success, making sales and profits, and most importantly generating a positive income for you and your family. You can start the BMG process even before you decide to leave the service; it applies anytime you want another stream of income, including earning a few hundred more a month. After achieving some success with BMG, then it's on to BP as the next stage of your business, and who you will target for your funding: Investors.

Business Planning is for businesses and investors

A business person writes a business plan, gets a loan from the bank or an investor, and tries to fill a niche in the local community. But if you do any research regarding businesses and business planning, you'll find that a number of successful companies never had a business plan. In fact, they followed the BMG approach in concept, although it wasn't called that until recently. Their basic business idea was jotted down on a bar or restaurant napkin, and then they went and did it (remember the need to act within five seconds of the idea!) and figured things out as they went along. Rarely is or was their idea formally written down. Doing a business plan is less of a requirement in today's startup market, but it can be very useful, if you've never had any business experience, to begin acquiring a business mindset.

If you do end up doing a business plan, it probably means your business has grown and needs outside investments for further growth—whether those investors are family, friends, Venture Capital (VC) or Angel Investors (AI). BP has always been intended to *attract investor funding for an already successful business.* The most frequent poor advice given to people wanting to start a business is: Do a business plan.

Scratch that! Follow the BMG model.

Below is a basic outline of what can be done regarding find funding for your business startup. These are not hard-and-fast rules, but basic ideas on what you find in the marketplace.

Business Investment Funding Levels

Funding Levels	Amount
Microfinance/Crowd Funding	<$10,000
True Angel	$10,000-50,000
Angel	$50,000-200,000
Individual Investors	$200,000-500,000
Collective Investors	$500,000-1,000,000
Venture Capitalist	>$1,000,000

One of the biggest mistakes entrepreneurs make regarding their business and approaching investors is expecting them to sign an NDA (Non-Disclosure Agreement) before talking with them. This is amateur hour. There are two things that investors look for:

- *Are you making sales and are you profitable?*
- *Can competitors duplicate what you're selling when you start getting very successful?*

When it comes to investors, what matters most is getting customers first, and patents and legal protection later. Why? Because ideas are a dime a dozen, i.e. basically worthless; it's all about execution. If you think about it, when brainstorming dozens of ideas, you might have a handful that are good, and one or two that are valid. The real value of an idea is in it execution: hustling and validating your business idea and model by making sales, being profitable, and have customers lined up to buy your product. It's when you hit profitability that both investors, and your competitors, will pay attention to you. That's when you write a business plan and line up investors.

Kevin: One of the questions I learned that helped change my business mindset is one that I now ask every person who wants to start a business to see where their head is: "If I gave you $1,000,000, what would you do with it?" Within a minute or two you can see whether or not they have a consumer or business/producer mindset. Those with the consumer mindset begin rattling off what they would spend the money, on versus those with a business/producer mindset who look to earn the money first with sales and increasing revenues. After I learned this lesson, I was interviewed and asked by a venture capitalist what I would have done with the money. I replied, "I'd give it back, because I'm not ready for any investment until I can prove my business can be successful and scalable."

25+ Businesses you can start for under $1,000

Whether contemplating a side-gig, side-hustle, or taking on a new passion project, you don't have to have thousands of dollars to start a business. Here are 25+ businesses that you can start for under $1,000:

- Personal chef
- Dog walker
- Tutor

- Tour guide
- Craftsman
- Accountant
- Caterer
- Personal trainer
- Property manager
- Wedding/event planner
- Au pair
- Copy editor/copywriter
- PR professional
- Personal shopper
- Freelance writer
- Graphic artist
- UI/UX designer
- Consultant
- Virtual assistant
- Makeup artist
- Transcriber
- Errand runner
- Photographer
- Translator
- Fashion stylist
- Professional organizer.

The above businesses can earn anywhere from $15-30/hour. You can also find out how much each of the businesses make via payscale.com to get an idea of not only what people pay, but more importantly, what your talents and skills are worth so you don't under-charge for your work or over-pay someone else.

Failure: When/where it is/is not an option

When RPGs are flying and you're in a critical military mission, failure is not an option—yet it can happen and sometimes does. We don't like missions to fail or service members to die, and are hardwired to do everything in our power to prevent failure. That means service members are driven for success. But in the civilian and business world, failure takes on a different meaning, and service members need to understand the differences, because it will determine how you move forward at each stage of your business growth.

In the civilian world, failure gets a mixed reaction. Some view failure as a career killer, while others see it as a stepping stone to success. In many lines of work in the civilian world, failure is a definite option—and at some level, a badge of honor. The simple fact is, in order to get to success, you may have to fail a number of times for improvement to occur. It's said that Thomas Edison tried well over 10,000 experiments before he perfected the incandescent lamp. When asked, "What would you have done if you had not finally uncovered the secret?" He replied, "With a merry twinkle in his eyes... 'I would be in my laboratory working now, instead of wasting my time talking with you.'"[43] You need to understand the meaning and word "failure" as it applies to business (and civilian life) and give it a different name and meaning: testing!

Testing. There's a familiar question that comes out of Silicon Valley: "Do you know what you call a twenty-something who has spent $5 million on a startup and failed? Experienced." In fact, the leadership expert and writer John C. Maxwell, in his book *Failing Forward,* says

---

[43] *A Year of Growing Rich* by Napoleon Hill, p. 126

that the average number of failed businesses successful millionaires have under their belts before they become successful is about five! Five businesses that they started and closed, and only *then* did these entrepreneurs became successful. What was common among every failure leading to success? Learning from their mistakes, and growing from taking these calculated risks.

This is an important concept to grasp, not only from an entrepreneurial/business aspect, but from an aspect of starting a new adventure. When you read the quips in Chapter 12, you'll hear from service members and veterans who were not quite prepared for transition for a variety of reasons. Read closely; take notes; let them give you insight so you can avoid the pitfalls they ran into. However, if somewhere along this transition you fail (financially, career/job-wise, emotionally, mentally, or physically), put a testing perspective on it. Being tested or testing the waters is a challenge to overcome; fail, and the challenge is done. Failure may not be an option, but testing is.

Action Plan: Continuing Your Mission

When it comes to having an action plan for your new adventure after your military service, it boils down to a few perspectives:

- Researching and understanding the importance of economics and the ever-changing marketplace, made up of both your clients and competitors.
- What talents, skills, and experiences do you have and need to grow into?
- Do you have the right mindset, support, and resources to move forward?
- Searching your marketplace niche for those that want or need your help, i.e. finding the right market product and service fit.
- ALWAYS know your business numbers—for example, sales and especially profit—and move from a part-time to a full-time business.
- Refer to the Business Model Generation methodology.

Notes:

_____

_____

_____

_____

_____

_____

_____

_____

_____

_____

_____

_____

_____

Notes:

_____

_____

_____

_____

_____

_____

_____

_____

_____

_____

_____

_____

_____

_____

9. Your Adventure in the Marketplace

Everyone has his own specific vocation or mission in life; everyone must carry out a concrete assignment that demands fulfillment. Therein he cannot be replaced, nor can his life be repeated; thus, everyone's task is unique as his specific opportunity to implement it. — Viktor E. Frankl

When the decision comes to getting out of the service, a natural first thought is: *what do I want to do with my life now?* Throughout this book, we've given you the resources to determine if you're ready to transition, resources to assist you in narrowing down your interests, and options to pursue those interests. Once you have at least narrowed down what you'd like to do and gathered some resources to pursue it, it's about searching for opportunities to make a living at your new mission. Earlier in the book, we discussed tips on networking. Now we'll dive a little deeper into the topic.

Marketing Yourself

The military has ingrained in us that a failure of one is a failure for everyone on the team. A cohesive team is responsible for the success of a mission. In the military, it's less about individualism, although there are individual standouts, and more about a cohesive whole and being a "quiet professional."

However, when you enter the civilian world as a veteran, you may go into an area that you may not be comfortable with—i.e. marketing or selling yourselves. The key is finding the balance between talking about the attributes you bring to the table versus feeling like you're bragging. This is why it is important to identify your military skills and translate them into terminology civilians can understand. The better you are at marketing your value for a business, the better chance you have of acquiring the position.

We touched on networking earlier in the book; now let's dive a little deeper into the variety of multiple lanes to take when connecting for a new adventure.

Social media platforms

Social media is just that: it's social, an electronic version of our physical selves. Facebook, Instagram, LinkedIn, Pinterest, Twitter, Google+... the list is long. While a veteran may use social media to connect with their various friends and connections, businesses and governments use it, too. They use it to connect with their customers, or as a part of their marketing, just as you use it to connect with friends and find work or a job.

Perception can be reality for some people. While businesses and governments are more conservative and careful, oftentimes *too* careful, about what they put in their social media accounts, veterans and potential job seekers may not be careful enough. Since it *is* social media, where both job and customer seekers may post something, inevitably what is posted may be construed as bad or even wrong. *Just be aware that both posting and not posting can both hurt and help you in your efforts*; it's all in the eyes and thoughts of those that are reading what you posted.

There are tons of social media sites where you can connect with others, but the top three social media sites for finding your next mission in life are listed below. The primary issue around social media is this: If you don't want your mother or grandmother to see it, then you surely don't want any potential employers to see it either, so keep it off the internet and social media. This goes not only for photos and videos, but things you might say on social media that could be construed the wrong way by others. Any negative post that is offensive to someone is one thing, but it is quite another when posting something that might get you in employment hot water.[44] Most hiring managers are using social media to get a more holistic view of the person and want to get a peek into a candidate's side interest in graphic design or volunteer work at a local hospital – items outside the confines of a normal résumé.

The purpose of social media for you, your work, or your business is to *support your efforts* to find work and to earn a living, not *to take the place* of finding work. Although many Fortune 500 and other companies are spending thousands and millions of marketing dollars for social media sites, their results show that fewer sales come from social media. In a business setting, social media does a much better job at *sales support* than actually increasing sales. If the Fortune 500 companies see these results, you bet veterans should take notice of their results and follow their lead. Learn the hard lessons from the money *they* spend, and not your own time and money.

What social media does is allow the veteran, organizations, and others to find each other 24/7/365, and make connections with no borders to cross or flights to catch. Your actions to find work during the day, making calls or contacting with other organizations to find work, should be your first priority upon leaving the service. Using social media to your advantage can enhance the process.

LinkedIn.com

After networking with other service members and veterans, your next area of connecting is through social media sites, and the first place

---

[44] time.com See *10 Social Media Blunders That Cost a Millennial a Job — or Worse*

to stop is the professional online résumé service, LinkedIn.com. LinkedIn is like "speed dating" for professionals. Some 93% of hiring managers search LinkedIn for recruits. Rule Number One about your LinkedIn profile is this: It should be public.

In the past, Human Resources would get the résumé you sent them and then ask you for and call your references to verify who you were. Today, with social media, searching via Google brings up all sorts of information about who you are that both you and friends have posted, on sites from Facebook through Pinterest to LinkedIn. That means the most important part today is for how you appear in a Google name search result, less about how your résumé looks (anyone or any company can download a PDF copy of your LinkedIn profile/résumé 24/7). Your LinkedIn bio should include title, industry and location, and *use keywords, not buzzwords*—think Search Engine Optimization (SEO)[45] here. If you have gaps in your work history, volunteer or do consulting work to fill such gaps.[46]

Within LinkedIn, you will find LinkedIn Groups. These are a great way to search for your potential targeted companies and work environment. Connect with as many groups as you can and then contribute to their forums to get your name in front of those who work in the organization you want to work in, as well as recruiters who see your name. Face-to-face is the best way to connect, but screen-to-screen via Skype, other videoconferencing technology, or through social media with someone on the other side of the Internet can be just as powerful.

---

[45] SEO is the process of affecting the visibility of a website or a web page in a web search engine's unpaid results—often referred to as "natural", "organic", or "earned" results.

[46] marketwatch.com. See *How job recruiters screen you on LinkedIn*

When it comes to your résumé, LinkedIn is fast and is an excellent source for having access to your résumé and professional information 24/7:

> *Create a traditional résumé and upload it to the Summary section of your LinkedIn profile as a media attachment. And yes, I would always be directing people to your LinkedIn profile when they're considering hiring you. Obviously, that's a good reason to make sure your profile is fully optimized.*—Kevin Knebl, Social Selling & Relationship Marketing Specialist

Facebook

To a lesser degree, there's Facebook. There is nothing wrong with having a Facebook personal or business account. Just keep in mind: in the search for hiring the right person, many companies will look to see if there are any "unhealthy or inappropriate" photos, videos, or posts in your social media. So, if you're starting to apply for jobs, it would behoove you to make sure there is nothing that could lead to misperceptions... and to keep that privacy setting such that you can control who sees what and when.

Your own web site

Don't think you need a web site? You might. It's not essential, but is can be important. If you want others to find you and any business you want to start, having your own web site for about $100-200/year is a great way for someone to find you 24/7/365. If you plan on having your own business or additional income streams (highly recommended), do consider starting this up as soon as possible. A web site doesn't have to be overkill and become a Swiss Army knife in its design (don't follow the mantra, "go big or go home"). Start simple, with basic information and content, and one of the many themes that come free and built-in with WordPress (be wary of other "free" themes, as they could include bad or malicious code or poor security that can hurt you). No need to purchase much in the beginning.

Once you've "gone live" with your web site, observe your site's traffic. Now find other sites that cater to the customer and content that you have an interest in, and start guest-blogging and writing content or posting forum comments that will then point back to your own web site. Normally, every comment requires three things: your name, email address, and website. Posting on other sites with good comments drives traffic to your site for those who are interested in what you have to say or offer. Your web site is intended to be a source to generate sales leads for your business.

Other social media sites

There are many other social media sites[47] that attract people for a variety of reasons.

- **YouTube** - A video-sharing social media site that is owned by Google, with more than 48 hours of new video uploaded to the site every minute.
- **Twitter** - A microblogging site where posts consist of 140 characters or less and are organized via hashtags (#), like #military, #iraq, #usmc, #navy, or just plain #veteran.
- **Pinterest** - A vision or theme-based board social photo sharing site to quickly share interests that are visually appealing.
- **Quora** - A question-and-answer website where questions are asked, answered, edited and organized by its community of users.

Be aware that hashtags (#) started with Twitter, but have been adopted by other social media and web sites; but limit how many you use in a post.

---

[47] wikipedia.org See List of a large number of social networking websites

Social media networking

Networking is still the best solution to finding work, hands down. Personal networking works especially well because it's face-to-face; however, social media isn't too far behind. It's readily accessible and breaks down barriers of both time and geography. Earlier, we talked about general networking tips. Now let's talk about tips when using social media to network.

1. Validate, validate, validate! Rule #1—what you see online may not be real. When you make a connection, do your research. Make sure you know if the information you are receiving is legitimate.

    Kevin: I was sent a LinkedIn message from someone I did not know personally and had no social media connection with at all. They sent a message explaining their cause and wanted me to become an investor. I found it odd that they were looking for a handout before they ever reached out with handshake to build a relationship. I replied to their email with those comments and while they thanked me for the feedback, the never took me up on my advice to connect and establish a relationship. Although I never found out specifically, the odds are high that this was a scam.

2. **Prioritize who matters most on your social network.** Once you have determined which individuals/organizations are genuine, list and determine the "critical few" out of your plethora of people, organizations, or social network platform/groups that you could talk to and connect with them. Work your "Top 10" social connections and then select your next top 10, and work them until you have gone through your

169

list. When something "hits," pour some more effort into what is getting traction.

3. **Polish the profile.** As you start do your research, others will start looking at you more. Make sure your professional networking sites have a professional picture and current résumé.

4. **Don't be overzealous.** When you make a promising contact, don't overdo the follow ups. Give them time to follow through with what they said they would. If they say they will get back with you in two days, follow up with them on day four or five.

5. **Think abundance, not scarcity.** Too often, a scarcity attitude (I win/you lose, I have/you don't, I get/you won't) on either side of an exchange comes across as desperate, small-thinking, ungrateful, and selfish, and gives off a bad vibe in a new social network relationship. It's important to keep in the forefront of your mind the idea that there's enough room for everyone to do their thing. Some of the most successful people are those who lead with gratitude and a pay-it-forward attitude. (Wait until you meet Mitch Durfee in the next chapter!)

6. **Think people, not positions.** It's all about relationships, and sometimes, when we're connecting through technology, it's easy to lose sight of the fact that there is an actual person on the other side. You wouldn't walk up to someone of the opposite sex the first time you met them and ask them to marry you, would you? Probably not; you'd get to know them first. Same with looking for work via social media. Get to know who you are connecting with. If they are in your area, meet up with them in a public place (safety first!) and get to know them. See

others as people first, not as contacts who can help you get what you want.

7. **"Thank you" still goes a long way.** Most people are willing to help other people without expecting anything in return. However, a sincere "thank you" is one of the best gifts one can give. It can be an email, a handwritten note, face-to-face, or even a gesture. For example, writing an online review on a product or business someone owns; giving positive feedback on their professional networking page, such as LinkedIn; or linking them with contacts you have that would assist them in pursuing their goals.

Moving forward with your new adventure

Okay: so here we are at the end of a lot of information. We hope you make this book look like a three-year-old ambushed it with highlighters and sticky notes. Please go back and re-read parts that you found pertinent (of course we hope that's most the book!). This is all for you. No gimmicks, no hidden agendas; just as much information as we could pack into a book in a stepped sequence that builds toward the final day you hang up your uniform and begin anew—not with both feet in the military, but one foot in the military and one in civilian life, looking forward to your new adventure.

But what good is this information unless we have validation from more than one transitioned veteran (Kevin) and one service member who sees the need for this book (Donna)? The next two chapters are full of tips, quips and stories from those with experience: veterans who have transitioned or are going through transition. They and the many others not mentioned in this book are the ones you need to connect with, listen to, and take advice from. The final chapter is a list of resources to assist you as you prepare for your next adventure. This new adventure you're embarking on is not a destination where you will arrive, i.e., "I have transitioned," but a journey with many stops along the way.

So sit back with your favorite beverage and enjoy the rest of this book.

Action Plan: Marketing Yourself

- Identify and translate your skill set.

- Check your social media for photos and comments that could be misconstrued.

- Utilize a variety of social media to assist you in searching for a position.

- Remember: social media is to assist in marketing yourself/your business and making connections that could lead to work or a new career in your new adventure.

Notes:

_____

_____

_____

_____

_____

_____

_____

_____

_____

_____

_____

_____

_____

_____

Notes:

_____

_____

_____

_____

_____

_____

_____

_____

_____

_____

_____

_____

_____

_____

10. Success Story - Warrior to Patriot Citizen

It is the soldier, not the reporter, Who has given us freedom of the press.
It is the soldier, not the poet, Who has given us freedom of speech.
It is the soldier, not the organizer, Who gave us the freedom to demonstrate.
It is the soldier, Who salutes the flag, Who serves beneath the flag.
And whose coffin is draped by the flag, Who allows the protester to burn the flag. —Father Dennis Edward O'Brien, USMC

Okay, so we've gone from A to Z, soup to nuts, top to bottom... whatever you want to call it. We've covered a lot of information. Now, to put it all together. Does it work? We've shown that George Washington was a historical personage who reflects what each veteran is capable of doing. We revealed the steps necessary for you to transition from serving in the military into your next mission in civilian life by following your talents and passions. The next step is validation of this information with an example. The following true story demonstrates what looking ahead, knowing your desires, developing a game plan, and following through—mixed with a little mitigated risk—will get you.

Veteran Success Story: Grunts Move Junk

Mitch Durfee is a young, energetic entrepreneur and the owner of Grunts Move Junk (gruntsmovejunk.com) in Burlington, Vermont. He is also a veteran. Specialist Mitch Durfee spent three years USA and two years USAR in Mechanized Infantry, Air Defense, and instructing. He was attached to the 5/5 ADA – 2nd Infantry Division out of Camp

177

Hovey, Korea and 3/61 Cav – 2nd Infantry Division, and involved in both Operations Phantom Fury and Iraqi Freedom. He is a great example of deciding it was time to move on, having a game plan, implementing the game plan, overcoming potentially limiting factors, and starting up what has become a continually growing business.

Coming from a family with a strong military background—a grandfather in the Navy, and his father and sister both in the Army—Mitch saw it as his civic duty to follow family tradition and join the Army the day after he turned 17. He knew right away he wanted Mechanized Infantry. "I wanted to be overseas. I wanted to have that pride, achievement kind of thing... to be able to be that guy who can put God, country and community ahead of everyone else." His plan was to complete a 20-year career; however, after being deployed for the first two years, career sticking points—and the physical impact of his work—made him start to realize that there were other things out there in the world that he wanted to explore.

I don't know... there's a lot of injuries just to my feet. They're worn out from carrying all the equipment. Being Mechanized Infantry overseas, you're on a vehicle... you're not walking around a lot, but when you lower the gate and go outside the gate, you're running through town 12 hours steady, kicking doors in with 80-100 pounds' worth of gear on you. There were days we were doing two- and three-day missions. I can remember running through these towns and my feet feeling like I was stepping on razors... like plantar fasciitis. Over time, my arches just started to collapse. There were those and the IEDs that were going off—they could kind of ring your bell. So I got a little PTSD, plantar fasciitis, dislocated my shoulder, probably from kicking in doors. You're not supposed to use your shoulder kicking in doors, but there's certain things you do when you're 20 years old; you just jump off the tank, you don't think about it, you're in the moment, it's like "Here we go."

Although the physical impact was intense, it wasn't the primary factor that lead him to getting out of the military.

> *It was just weighing the options of "Hey, look, been in for three years now, I can stay in for another three years." But the MOS I originally went into, I re-classed two times in three years. And also, in combination, I couldn't get promoted because the military was shifting over at a certain point in time... certain MOS's were getting promoted ahead of me, and it was difficult to see my peers getting promoted when I was trying to be the model soldier; trying to do the perfect APFT test, the perfect on-the-range kind of thing. You want to be that elite solider, but even though I was doing those things, I still couldn't get promoted just based on certain scores. You needed to have a 798 perfect score, college degree, perfect on your APFT, perfect on everything across the board just to get promoted. So, at that point in time I kind of juggled, Hey, look, I can either stay a specialist for the next three years until I finally re-class," which I didn't want to go back through training and then coming up three months later they were going back overseas and it's like, all right, I don't want to spend another year overseas; I can't get promoted even if I go overseas. So, at this point in time it was better for me to step out.*

However, going "cold turkey" didn't happen. He lasted a month after transitioning and then decided to join the Reserves, thinking he would keep it as a lifeline to get back to active duty if necessary. Instead, he found the Reserves to be a completely different beast, and eventually got out of the military altogether. It was a bittersweet parting.

> *I have always believed that ABC means not only Above and Beyond the Call of Duty, but it also means that people that go above and beyond should be rewarded for their efforts and not be used up like a resource. I*

was proud of my service and wanted to complete the marathon, but after being pulled around in so many directions, it felt like I was never going to get what I felt I deserved from the career in the service, from Air Assault to Special Forces, to choice of duty station. I didn't want to wait around hoping I would get those opportunities.

Transition came with its own struggles. Although Mitch made the choice to get out for career opportunity reasons, his medical issues did have an impact on the civilian side. But Mitch's positive outlook and moving-forward attitude has allowed him to "adapt and overcome" many hurdles.

Losing a couple good friends over there was really tough. Being at a younger age, I think I didn't handle it as well as some of the other guys that were older and more mature, because they were more mentally developed. I think that when I was really young, instead of taking it at face value… there was an emotional rollercoaster… there were days I just didn't want to go on… so there were those challenges. But most of the time I combated those thoughts with just being engulfed with starting a business. If I slowed down, it was worse. So, if I had time to actually sit down on the back deck, just thinking, or I was lying in bed for a day, that is when the thoughts were worse. What slowly started happening was, okay, I'm working a normal job, I go home and I'm watching TV, and I was like "Okay, these thoughts are back"… and I was seeking help through the VA and going to counseling for a lot of those kind of things. But over time, I realized if I'm just working until I'm completely tired and crawl in the shower, rinse off, crawl into bed, wake up early ready to start the next day… there really wasn't time to think about those thoughts. So that helped, I think, with getting businesses going.…

180

Mitch knew two things he wanted to do when he got out—go to college and start a business. No matter; going out into the "unknown" civilian world, he had apprehensions.

When I got out the service, it was much like leaving any other career you've worked at for three years. You're unsure of where to go next. The major difference is with the end of the military career, you are also out of touch of the network you had three years before you left. This is why the GI Bill and going to college was a great stepping-stone. It helped me get an education, while also assisting me in developing a network for job placement. The College Road Map and GI Bill are amazing programs, but it was never the end-all solution to finding a career. I used my spare time to work towards developing business models.

Mitch felt the military was an asset for going to college. "The military really teaches soldiers in general certain values that other colleges fail to give – loyalty, duty, respect, selfless service, integrity, personal courage." He graduated from St. Leo's in St. Leo, Florida in 2011 with a degree in Liberal Arts, combined with a slew of business courses from a variety of other colleges. Mitch then set out to fulfill his second goal: starting a business. He wasn't sure exactly what he wanted to do. He knew that finding people who had the same work ethics and mindset as his fellow veterans was going to be a key to his success.

I had that lifeline of being able to go back active if I really wanted to. But I wanted to start a business. After being overseas and doing all that stuff, it just seemed in my life where it was, "Hey, let's meet every Sunday with all my best friends" to try to get them to come up with business ideas… We started a hundred different businesses, and it was more like just learning what we needed to do to get a business going. When you walk

181

into a store and see that guy behind the counter at Sears or something, going the extra mile and he's still working at Sears because he doesn't [know] the next place to go... He doesn't have a resource to lift him to the next level. You walk in there and he's like, "Hey, how are you today. What are you looking for?" And not only does he do that, he follows you through the store and gets you what you need and then goes that extra mile. I always saw people like that as guys who really should have an opportunity to be more successful. I thought if I could find those guys and surround myself with them and create a model that gave those guys opportunities to be successful, then there is no way it wouldn't be successful. And those come hand-in-hand, working with military guys. I knew a lot military guys who had more drive. When we were in the military, we walked road marches for 15-20 miles or so, and some guys that do it, when they get done they're like, "That's it? Okay, let's keep going." If you can get your hands on people like that, there's no reason why you can't be successful.

Before he jumped into his own start-up, Mitch worked for Pepsi in quality control, and found it was more give than receive. This led him to start his transition to working for small businesses. Blazing Designs (a fireplace company) and Urban Gorillas (military training bodies) were two small businesses he worked for, where he learned the beauty and benefits of being an entrepreneur. This gave him the confidence to start his own business. Mitch is a great example of using the skills you developed in the military and finding your own path to success. He tried the traditional routes of start-up help—Small Business Administration, banks, and business-plan writing workshops.

For him, it was just getting out there and getting sales. "Although it gives you a road map, don't spend too much time worrying about getting a business plan perfect unless you're looking for investors." He found his tenacity was his biggest skill asset when it came to starting a business.

> *One of the most important skills "vetpreneurs" have is the lack of ability to give up when times get tough! There will always be ups and downs, but the "take no excuse for mission failure" attitude resides in most vets. When you quit making excuses for why you're failing and spend that energy to coming up with a solution, success is only a few more steps to go, so keep going!*

To hear Mitch talk, it seems natural to assume that he's pursuing his passion; and on some level, he is. However, when asked if he has *found* his passion, it's not so black-and-white to him.

> *Geez, I think the guys will kill me if I say no. For a business to be successful, you have to be passionate about it. There is no doubt that without a little bit of passion in what you're doing, you can't be successful. So I would say the success comes from the passion we have. It's not the picking things up or the cleaning up that I'm passionate about. It's giving back to the community; building your own little group of guys that can add to something, like... I guess the best way to say it is, if you have a giant rock wall, one person can't push the wall over. It takes two, three, four, five guys to get this thing rolling... and that is why when building this team of people that want to be to be successful it really transitions to, "Hey look, I want to be successful, but I can't be successful on my own; and you want to be successful, and now we have some momentum." It's the third, fourth, fifth, sixth guys that really create that movement, that really get each one of us to the level of success we all imagine us being at... and that is what I am passionate about. I am passionate about all of us being successful, because that was the original goal. Anyone can be successful in a career they enjoy, but [to be] able to reach mountaintops of success, you*

have to have passion for the product or service you have. I love being able to help put veterans back to work and I love being able to continue to help serve our community. But my true passion I haven't completely unveiled yet.

However, as you listen to him, it becomes obvious that real estate, helping others, and connecting with and giving back to the community are part of his "unveiled" talents and passion. You'll find him hanging out at 14th Star Brewery (14thstarbrewing.com) while listening to Jazz Entertainment (Jazevt.com), both military owned businesses. "So after we're done working, the next thing we do, we go support another military business because it's lifting everyone to the next level." He gushes about game plans that would assist veterans transitioning to the civilian world, better the community, and just make the world he engages in a little better.

Finding your passion... geesh... I wish I had an answer for that. Grunts Move Junk is an amazing group of guys and girls that put everything on the table and go the extra mile. But my passion, I don't know... real estate. I want to own a lot of real estate. I want to also be able to give back to the communities. And that is why I think that Grunts works so well. I get to see houses, I get to help people sell their houses. I get to bring the community... from all of Vermont... make greening it up... you see all of these properties that are kind of rundown. And if I had it my way, if I could get the state to grant us the money to make this house look better while also employing veterans, which is kind of a no-brainer. Why would you not want to give jobs to other veterans? You know, we always try to take care of each other... my best friend, Jon Peterson, I helped get him overseas with me to Afghanistan, and when he got back he was kind of struggling between jobs and everything. So we flew him up there and now he's not looking for a job anymore and he is able to

184

do Grunts while still attending college because we are really flexible with that. We understand education is important, and we also give him the opportunity to hopefully start his own business. He wants to start a marketing business, which works hand-in-hand with what we do. We can kind of train him on how we are marketing, and then also teach him how to get customers.

Donna: Is that how you see Grunts operating in the future, as sort of taking people who are just coming out and helping them to transition to something else?

Yeah, I think originally that was the idea. Grunts Move Junk is a low-bearing entry model... anyone can be a mover. You pick things up and put things down; anyone can do landscaping; anyone can do junk removal— you just need a pickup truck. But really what it comes down to is, the best way to find a job is to have a job. You know, guys get out of the military and there are employers that will really understand this. "Oh cool, you have a résumé here. It looks like you've spent six months unemployed. Can you explain that?" "Well, I served in Iraq/Afghanistan; I came back to a town where I didn't know anyone. I didn't have a place to live, had to get back on track." So, it was, "Yeah, we'll give you a job. Come on in. When can you start? Can you start tomorrow? Perfect. Let's get you in the uniform and let's get you back with peers and we will slowly transition you to the field that you want to be in." Because we do so much, from moving to landscaping, construction, marketing, sales—it's all kind of under the same umbrella. We just take those guys and we can write them a nice letter of recommendation and get them in to the careers they want... We've had guys that came back and we had them for 2-3 months and we put them into the electrical field as an apprentice. So yeah, as we scale up across the country, it would be great to take these guys and give them a paycheck and an opportunity to be around their peers as they transition.

Donna: It sounds like what I'm hearing you saying is that these people coming out of the military are already hired by you. They already have the application: it was the military.

Exactly. I mean, if you serve, then we will definitely sit down with you. We do have really high standards, but most of the guys that served honorably and got out are pretty much qualified. You see that with a lot of government positions, too. So, if you got out of the military and you wanted to work for Border Patrol or Customs or any of those government organizations, you get a preference. And there is a reason for that: because you really understand the business model. The CEO is just the commander, so it's the same type of transformation. Just as you climb in rank in the military, you climb in rank in business. And the quick transfer is a different uniform and different hours… you get to sleep in and you get to go home early.

Donna: So with what you have now in your life –the real estate and Grunts—what are you most passionate about in the scope of those two things?

Passion for real estate, that really gets my blood moving. I don't know what it is. For one, you get to meet a ton of people, and there's the rush of winning that negotiation, also being able to help your client get the value out of what they are looking for. Being able to be that tool that helps them be successful… I like that, and I also like to own it. Who doesn't like to own it, looking out the window and say, "That's mine"? With Grunts being able to say, "Hey look, I served, I know you served… I want to take care of you because I know the struggles you're in, because 10 years ago my struggles were just as tough. Let me hopefully be able to take care of you."

Being a business owner/entrepreneur, Mitch has the luxury of setting the vision. One thing Mitch prides himself on is basing his company's foundation on the same foundation as the military. He recognizes that it sets his company part from other civilian businesses, and goes on to explain the differences he sees in the military versus civilian sector.

The Grunts are based off the same foundation as the military… but in the civilian world it is who's been here longer that matters. It's the good old boys system, it seems like. You walk in and you may be qualified, but if you don't know the person sitting behind that desk who is going to hire you, then you really have to work at getting that spot or you are going to start at the bottom and climb. The military may also be a little bit like that, but the military also has set standards to get you to the point to be promotable.

Looking back to his years in the military and his transition, Mitch can reflect upon the good/bad and offer advice for those new to the military and those transitioning out. For those new to the military:

Build your network; don't piss anyone off. You're in the military, you know you are hard-bodied, you're hot-headed, you're young, but don't let that cloud your vision… enjoy the time that you are in, because that group of people, you are going to have that bond the rest of your life. The guys that I met in basic training I still stay in touch with almost 12 years later. I'm still chatting and seeing the guys, too. With Grunts, we travel across the country and I can still call those guys up and say, "Hey look, I'm coming through NC this weekend, can I crash on your couch?" "Yeah, let's go out, we'll have a drink." So it's nice to be able to see these guys you met all around the world and still meet up with them.

And for those transitioning out,

Get that résumé on spot. It's a challenge... even myself, I went three to six months unemployed during that gap, and there is really no way to bridge it, because even when I came back from Afghanistan this last time, I had a game plan in mind: I'm going to come back and do this... and it was like, well, I thought I would be able to find a job a little quicker than this. Don't give up... looking for a job is a full-time job. You can't just kind look for a job and say "Yeah, I'm here to work." It's just like any other sales thing—follow up, follow up, follow up. So if you really want that job and you know it's what you're going to do, start making those calls, start following up with them, saying "Hey look, I'm going to be transitioning out," or go to college. Plan your exit on a college date so you can at least get into college and ride that. There is [a network of veterans that hire people]... there are definitely sites out there that are affiliated with that. There are a lot of different vet franchises, that if you did want to start your own business you could look for franchises that are vet-friendly and offer discounts and stuff like that. That's kind of a good model too, so if you are looking to start your own business, franchising makes it a lot easier.

Grunts has been in business for under two years, and continues to grow. Today you can find Mitch doing any number of tasks – on-site moving "junk," day-to-day operations, sales, marketing, answering emails, or crafting leaders. Focusing on building leaders is something he blocks out time for.

188

Once a week, I meet with certain team leads to say, "Hey look, where are you at with your goals now; where do you want to be? Are you still staying true to your goals? Do you need to block out time to make sure this is what is going on, then do it?" I've gained a lot of experience in the last 16 months, and I want to be able to give that experience to the guys as they join the team.

Reflecting on his various military events and injuries, he acknowledges there was good that came out of all of it.

I think that if the physical and mental injuries that I got overseas never happened, I would have stayed in the military, and I think I would have ridden the 20-year wagon. I think that because there were those events in my life at such a young age... well, I did want to start a business, but that was postponed... it was when I was 38. Hey, I'll figure something else out, I'll get a second retirement at the end. But it wasn't because I wasn't able to keep to the standards of the military; you know, I could still do the AFPT test today, and I could still crush it. It was more so that those events and just being, I would say, 'used,' used as a resource... they just used me up as a resource. If that had never happened I would have stayed in for 20, but because of those injuries I had two choices... go find a civilian job where I could work 9 to 5 and work until I'm 65, or be self-employed so I can still stay on track toward my goal of wanting to retire at 38. So, when I say I want to retire at 38, that means that I have to take responsibility for my own future, and you know there is no small business around that is going to have a retirement plan set up so you can retire by the time you are 38.

At the end of the day, Mitch is a thriver. His ability to keep thinking forward has allowed him to determine the right time for him to leave the service, prepare an educational and financial game plan for transition, and pursue what he felt drawn to, entrepreneurship. His experience is exactly what George Washington and previous veterans did, and what most future veterans will do after their service: They press on. Any new path one takes is never a straight line, as others might perceive it. It curves around obstacles, moves through events, and twists through the challenges life brings to us as it happens. But intertwined into the core of his business is ensuring his brothers- and sisters-in-arms have a plan – whether it be working at Grunts or having Grunts become a stepping-stone for their future endeavors. Mitch has had to overcome obstacles, but has done it in a constructive way that benefits not only him and his business, but includes looking out for the individuals that work for the company as well as an entire community.

Update: It has been over a year since the interview with Mitch, and he has continued to move onward and upward. He has opened his second Grunts Move Junk location and has been asked to open in three more locations. He still loves real estate, and has aligned himself on a team where he can focus more on the marketing and investment side of the house.

During his interview, Mitch still had not determined what his true passion was. After starting Grunts and continuing exploring real estate, he figured it out. It is the branding, marketing and funneling of customers to businesses. In response to identifying his passion, he established a new company: Online Start Up Box (onlinestartupbox.com). The start-up utilized creative ways to connect brands and customers. The sky is the limit for Mitch Durfee, and he is a prime example of how luck (preparation + opportunity) can lead to finding one's passion in life.

Notes:

_____

_____

_____

_____

_____

_____

_____

_____

_____

_____

_____

_____

_____

_____

_____

_____

Notes:

_____

_____

_____

_____

_____

_____

_____

_____

_____

_____

_____

_____

_____

_____

_____

11. Veteran's Quips, Advice, and Letters

The truth of the matter is that you always know the right thing to do. The hard part is doing it.—General Norman Schwarzkopf

We could write tips for a successful transition and finding your talents and passions all day, but none of it would be of any real value unless we had validation from those who have already been through, or are currently going through, the process. We've interviewed service members from all ranks and all services to get their best advice. These are their responses to questions regarding transitioning; these are the stories told by veterans in their own words (with some minor editing for clarity or conciseness), but nothing is varnished here. So without further ado, grab a drink and a chair and let's begin.

Reasons for leaving

There comes a point in everyone's military service when they determine it's time to go. In our interviews, we found the decision was rarely anything to do with being tired of service, but rather a myriad of other reasons.

I injured my back and because I could no longer fly, I would never be promoted again.—*S.D., CW2 (ret), 26.5 years USA/Army ANG, Patton Tanker, Abrams Tanker, Apache Helicopter Repairer, Aircraft Electrical and Environmental Systems Repairer, Apache Helicopter Pilot.*

My mother was diagnosed with Alzheimer's and was in the final stages of the disease. She was living with me, and I was finding it harder and harder to work full-time and care for her. My aunt came to stay with me to help with her, but it still was not enough, and the resources for in-home care were very expensive. Putting her in a nursing home was not an option for me. She was a military spouse, following my father for 30 years and then following me around. It was time to give back to her for her service to us.—D.R., Col (ret), 31 years, USA, Military Intelligence Officer

Started my Ph.D.—W.P., E6 (sep), 11 years Navy/Army Reserves, Diver and Drill Sergeant

I was assigned in non-flying positions for the last three years of service.—R.W., CW4 (ret), 23 years 2 weeks, USA, Special Operations Pilot

I completed my initial enlistment. I wanted to give college a try.— J.B., Staff Sergeant (sep), 4 years USAF, Aircraft Loadmaster

Active Duty – separated March 1988 due to not enjoying my military career any longer. AF Reserves – left the reserves due to civilian position's working hours being too great to sustain any other employment. ANG – due to injuries sustained while activated, I am not physically healthy enough to sustain the rigors of what is required for a military career.— J.D., Staff Sergeant, 11 AD, 1 Reserve, 3 ANG Cyber System Operator.

Normal retirement; did not have to retire, but decided the timing was right for me and for my family.—K.C., Col (ret), 27 years, USA, Military Intelligence Officer

194

After one-year deployment in Iraq I'd had enough.—M.M., MSgt (ret), 24.5 years USAF, Independent Duty Medical Technician

I was almost retirement eligible and was going to retire in Germany where I was stationed; then I was unexpectedly promoted to O6 and forced to leave Germany after only one year in my job (17AF/SG2). The Colonel's Group decided I should go to San Diego and work in the (Navy run) TRICARE Regional Office-West as the Director, Business Operations. I had little to no expertise in the area... and worked for a GS 15 who had never been in the military and hated the Air Force. It soon became clear she hated me (thank goodness my staff loved me; otherwise I probably would've ended up on the NMCSD psych ward!), and took every opportunity to demonstrate her feelings (public humiliation in meetings with executives in Tri-West and DoD). So, when the AF offered a TIG (time in grade) waiver, I took it. I lost $500/month for the rest of my life by leaving early. —K.V., Col (ret), 24 years USAF, Health Service Administrator

Did not like the cultural change happening in the Navy, and the family wanted me to get out.—P.F., Chief Petty Officer, 23 years USNR, Gunner's Mate

Completed 20 years of service and did not want to retire in port, so declined an overseas assignment and dropped my papers to retire.—J.F., MSgt (ret) 20 years USAF, Computer Operations Supervisor

23 years of faithful service. It was time.—J.R., MSgt (ret), 23 years USA/USAFR, Army Combat Medic/Aerospace Medical Technician

End of hitch.—D.H., Petty Officer 2nd Class (ES), 4 years Navy, Court Reporter/Legal Clerk/Paralegal

Given injuries sustained, previous combat deployments and my last deployment, I felt my service, age, and desire for a "return to normalcy" to be deciding factors as to retirement.—G.P., LtCol (ret), 38 years 4 months USAF, ANG, USAFR, Medical Service Corps Officer.

Multiple events, but ultimately it was because I had the choice to do so.— J.G, SSgt, 16 years, USMC, USA, Rifleman/Mortarman/Infantryman

I felt I fulfilled all my expectations in the military and was not looking to become a squadron commander; budget issues also reduced or eliminated the IMA possibility.—M.G., Lt Col, 25.5 years USAR/USAFR, Construction Equipment Operator/Health Service Administrator.

Got out due to asthma and not being able to complete PT tests anymore.—W.H., Staff Sergeant, 11½ years USAF (sep), Aerospace Medical Journeyman

I found the place I wanted to retire to (from MacDill AFB, Tampa, Florida) and didn't want to PCS and then come back.—J.M, Maj (ret), 26 years USAF, Nurse

I could have stayed for 34 years, but at 32 years did not want to roll the dice and face a SERB (even if they [sic] would have SERB'ed me - I was finishing my second group command and was not a candidate for General). If I had been SERB'ed I would have to be out in 120 days. By choosing to retire, I had one year. So essentially, I decided to try something else.—Col, 32 years USAF, Aircraft Maintenance and Munitions

To enter the job market at a young age and have my skills and background drive my income.—M.S., Technical Sergeant, 11 years USAF, Medical Logistics

Preparing for transition

Ever hear the saying "Luck = preparation + opportunity"? Luck rarely just happens. Even to win the lottery, you have to buy the ticket first. There's no one right way to do it; do it the right way for you. Research, ask questions, network, ask more questions… be an expert in your future. No doubt the more prepared you are for the event, the better off you will be. The service members we interviewed agreed.

I connected with the world and did not have time to prepare for transition. Hard work, the will to never give up, persevere, and accept the challenges led to a little good luck and some open paths that have given me the opportunity to find my path to where I am today.—J.G., SSgt, 16 years, USMC/USA, Rifleman/Mortarman/Infantryman

When I left active duty, I went straight to college. I had trouble adjusting to civilian life and joined the Army Reserves.—W.P., E6, 4 years Navy, 7 years Army Reserves, Diver & Drill Sergeant

The first organization I reached out to was AMVETs. They were great in helping me prepare my paperwork for my disability… I recommend every person transitioning reach out to one of these organizations to help them. They know the system inside and out and will help you get what you deserve… Every transitioning service member should ensure they have a complete copy of all their military medical records. The next organization I contacted was RMOA (Retired Military Officers Association). They are a great contact to network with entrepreneurs, businesses, contractors, etc. They provide advice about what you needed to do to be competitive and stand-out in the civilian world. I reached out to other service members that were colleagues and friends for their advice and contact information. Many read my résumé to ensure it was up to date and the standards necessary to get a job. They also talked to me about the difference of applying for a government job versus a civilian job versus jobs for veterans. Also make a list of things to do, places to go, people to see and then ensure you do just that. Create a networking system. Get on-line into the various forum for transitioning.—D.R., Col (ret), 31 years USA, Military Intelligence Officer

I did not prepare for the transition. I only completed a résumé, but that was the extent of my transition. The U.S. Army offered transition training, but it was geared for Government Civilian Services. LinkedIn is a great resource for transitioning. I found the only way to find work in the field I wanted was to network to secure a job in [the] workforce.—R.W., CW4, 23 years 2 weeks USA, Special Operations Pilot.

I had a plan to go to college. I visited colleges and made arrangements on my own. That part was fairly easy because I started early. I separated in February, but colleges did not begin until September; six months. That was a difficult time, because I had to find a place to live and to make sure I did not erode all the money I had saved for college. Initially, I returned home, to Indiana, and lived with my parents. Unemployment was high, so I returned to Arkansas where I more easily found a job. For most of that time I moved in with some old Air Force buddies who lived off base. I slept on the floor the entire time there.—J.B., Staff Sergeant, 4 years USAF, Aircraft Loadmaster

Earned an MBA during my time in service; attended ACAP classes/résumé class at ACAP; began attending job fairs roughly 4 years out mostly as spectator for years 3&4 so I could learn before I was seriously seeking a job; bought interview clothes; collected résumés and intelligence from friends leaving or who had recently left the service; requested résumés from civilian friends to see what worked for them; networking; read a few books on résumés and interviewing.—K.E., CW4, 20 years USA, Apache Pilot.

The way I prepared was to gather my military training records, compile them and develop a résumé for civilian employment. I then used transition assistant resources to gather contact email address and phone numbers to hot call/contact recruiters in the area I wanted to relocate to. By using these channels, I was contacted by several contract houses and I was able to apply for positions I was interested in (all of them as I needed work). [The resources I used to assist with my transition were] networking with professional contacts, friends, relatives, friends of friends, job sites, USA Jobs and professional job placement organizations.—J.D., Staff Sergeant, 11 AD, 1 Reserve, 3 ANG Cyber System Operator.

I attended all services offered for retirees, sometimes twice. Had my military résumé translated into civilian language. Stayed connected with friends who were retired and built up my social network. [I used] websites, VAjobs.gov, Show Your Stripes.—M.M., MSgt (ret), 24.5 years USAF, Independent Duty Medical Technician

I prepared for my transition by completing my college degree in Computer Science and worked with the Separations team in base administration. I did not connect with anyone in the civilian world, other than to submit résumés and request interviews. Twenty years ago, the Internet was in its infancy so it wasn't much help. There was no LinkedIn or other large networking resources. The base had a listing of employers who had registered with the Armed Forces, so I used that to start sending out my résumés. The base also offered a separation support group and training in interviewing.—J.F., MSgt (ret), 20 years USAF, Computer Operations Supervisor

The last assignment I took while on active duty was to transition into a civilian instructor position on Ft. Hood. I was in a fortunate position to be aware of the transition from soldier instructors to civilian instructors, and was able to fill the civilian position once my discharge was official. The best resources were other veterans who had already walked the transition path. The briefings, literature and counselors present the "best case" scenario. But when you talk to other vets they give you the reality of how to maneuver when your circumstances veer from the "norm" and become unique.—J.R., MSgt (ret), 16 years USA/8 years USAFR.

[My] ultimate goal while in [the] service was to attend college. Upon discharge, I enrolled in University. Fellow veterans at school [were very helpful with my transition.]—D.H., Petty Officer 2nd class, 4 years Navy, Court Report/Legal Clerk/Paralegal

I had little preparation for my actual retirement, although I had been investing and planning for lifestyle changes for some time. The VA answered my medical needs post my last deployment and retirement; the USAF AD did not; I believe as a USAFR Officer they were not going to expend time and energy toward my injuries.—G.P., Lt Col (ret), 38 years, 4 months, USAF, ANG, USAFR, Medical Service Corps Officer

I decided last year after I realized there were no real MSC [Medical Service Corp] deployment possibilities in Europe and my attempt at IMA positions the year before a "dud," that this was [the] time to transition. As a VA employee working at the TRICARE regional office, I consider myself a SME in transition and therefore provide guidance to those assisting ADSMs [active duty service members] or those in direct contact in the process. I am not able to say fully that I will not need any resources, as I have not been retired that long. I expect I will not need any resources by relying on my comrades who have retired over the last few years for guidance.—M.G., Lt Col (ret), 3.5 years USAR, 22 years USAFR, General Construction Equipment Operator, Health Service Administrator

Didn't have a chance to prepare. From the time I failed my last PT test to the time I was out was three weeks.—W.H. (sep), 11½ years USAF, Aerospace Medical Journeyman

Being a nurse, I made applications to every hospital in the area before I was to go on terminal leave. The transition office at MacDill AFB helped me translate my military accomplishments into a résumé that civilians could understand. I interviewed, while on terminal leave, accepted a position before terminal leave ended, and was double-dipping for a while.—J.M., Maj (ret), 26 years USAF, Nurse

I connected with others who had retired before me and were in influential positions in large aviation companies. Executive TAP was useful in building résumés and gave me the skills to leverage contacts.— Col (ret), 32 years USAF, Aircraft Maintenance and Munitions

Separating comes with a few more challenges, as there is no financial buffer of the retirement check. The service members we interviewed who chose to separate took many factors into consideration before making their final decision.

[Factors I took into consideration were] where I wanted to live; salary I would need to support my family; finding a job that I wanted to do; assuring I had job secured prior to transition; benefits that would be lost if I separated; evaluating long term goals in regards to my professional career; how family would adapt to change.—M.S., TSgt, 11 years USAF, Medical Logistics

Education, Freedom, Organic vs Mechanistic Culture, the ability to pursue my own talents.—J.G., SSgt, 16 years, USMC/USA, Rifleman/Mortarman/Infantryman

The focus of this book is pursuing talents and passions. Not everyone knows exactly what they want to do when they get out, but having a general idea of what stimulates your mind and gets you excited is a good start. When you have a good grasp of that, you have a direction. The service members we interviewed may not have necessarily followed what they considered their talents and passion, but did go in a direction that was of interest to them. The takeaway is to learn what they did to get into their civilian field of interest and apply it to pursuing your passion.

I was open to anything that would improve my quality of life. Naturally, I leaned towards a career that somewhat aligned with my military experience. Ten years later, I am still in procurement and supply chain management. I am no longer in the medical space, but being able to adapt and apply core principles of procurement I learned in the AF has allowed me to transition across multiple market sectors and now work in the oil and gas space for a super major. [The steps I took to get to the career I am currently in]: Continued to focus on education; ability to adapt and apply the 'whatever it takes' attitude; be open to learning new things and not stovepipe yourself into the exact career field I had in the AF;

networked with everyone I met; apply for every job that even somewhat related to my experience; be confident in my interviews and show the interviewer that if you didn't know something all they had to do is show me and I would not only learn it but do it well; always looked for next opportunity and fight the feeling I had to be loyal to the end with careers that did not get me to my goals financially or provide me with the work life balance I wanted; updated résumé for every job I applied for and tailored the focus of my CV to highlight skills and background specific to the job description.—M.S, TSgt, 11 years, USAF, Medical Logistics

I was looking for work in training and simulation, and yes, this job actually found me. I was contacted by an international recruiting firm after they saw my qualifications on LinkedIn.—SD, CW2, 26.5 years, USA, Apache Pilot/Repairer, Aircraft Electrical and Environmental Systems Repairer, Abrams/Patton Tanker

None really, I was offered the position before I left active duty because of my previous experience with the program.—B.O. CSM, 36 years, USA/USAR, Senior Engineer Sergeant

When I decided to get off active duty in 2001, there was an opportunity to get into the plumber's union in Chicago. I did and that has become my career.—P.F., Chief Petty Officer, 23 years USNR, Gunner's Mate

I did all the classes the Army required and all the medical stuff, etc. The biggest thing I did was write and continually polish my résumé, established/re-established my contacts, and kept in touch with people. Vitally important to let everyone know you are on the market.—K.C., Col 9ret), 27 years, USA, Military Intelligence Officer.

Continue to focus on learning and education

The goal of education is not necessarily about getting an official piece of paper with your name on it, but about continuing to learn and grow. It IS about finding the right content that will benefit your pursuit to your next adventure. Notice that both Steve Jobs and Bill Gates never finished college and became billionaires, but they also never stopped learning and growing as individuals, either.

I was contacted by an international recruiting firm after they saw my qualifications on LinkedIn. I love the job I'm doing now. It has just been a continuation of what I was doing for the Army during my last assignment. I made sure my LinkedIn account was always up to date and asked for recommendations from Commanders and co-workers—S.D., CW2, 26.5 years, USA, Patton Tanker, Abrams Tanker, Apache Helicopter Repairer, Aircraft Electrical and Environmental Systems Repairer, Apache Helicopter Pilot

Since I retired from the National Guard and not from Active Duty, my plan to start my own business is still there, but waiting for my retirement and VA compensation to kick in so I will have the time and money it will take to start it. So I am currently working as a defense contractor in a program I helped create during one of my previous assignments on active duty and I am still working directly with the military so it was a very easy transition.—B.O., CSM, 36 years USA, AANG.

I found that most flying positions are underpaid and companies are willing to accept a person with less experience over paying more for an experienced pilot. [It is] not really a passion. Having a career in an interesting industry does help, but may not pay the bills. Your objectives should be clearly defined as you search for a follow-on career. I created my position, updated my résumé and LinkedIn profile, started a website and became involved in the industry by attending conventions and networking with businesses. It was through this approach I landed a job. I am the Vice President of Science and Technology for my company. I chose this job as opposed to unemployment, but expect to cultivate this into a passion.— R.W. CW4 (ret), 23 years 2 weeks USA, Special Operations Pilot.

[I did not know] exactly [what career I wanted to pursue], but I realized even before transition that I was unlikely to find another job that offered the same satisfaction as the Army, but I could try to get close. [I] established/re-established my contacts and kept in touch with people. Vitally important to let everyone know you are on the market. I found a really good small firm with people I like. The president offered me a job and I was thankful to get it, so here I am. No regrets at all, this is the good life.—K.C., Col (ret), 27 years USA, Military Intelligence Officer

Yes, [I am pursuing my passion]. I am the owner of a company that started in my basement to grow to over 100 employees, providing services around the world. I like running my own business and there is no rank to dictate the degree to which I can excel and achieve. [I] worked as a Project and Program Manager for a couple of small businesses and learned from those experiences and became knowledgeable of federal government contracting by reading and studying as well.—W.G., MSgt (ret), 21 years USMC, Administrative logistics management/SIGINT Support

Best and worst advice

Best advice was to ensure I did everything I needed to do medically. I don't think I got any bad advice. All advice is good, some better than others.—D.R., Col (ret), 31 years USA, Military Intelligence Officer

Best advice: Don't give up, reinvent yourself, invest in your Brand, network. Worst Advice: Take any job until the right one comes along.— R.W., CW4(ret), 23 years 2 weeks USA, Special Operations Pilot

Best: I was uncertain I could succeed in college. A Captain I served with assured me I could succeed in college. He encouraged me to at least give it a try. He told me I could always return to the Air Force if college didn't work out. I was literally told to "Aim High," to not underestimate what I could do. I doubted it, but he was right. I think when soldiers, sailors, and airmen separate, they can do a lot more in the civilian world than they realize. Adjusting is tough, but if they persist they will succeed. Worst: I had a few older Sergeants tell me I could not make it outside the Air Force, that it would be "stupid" to give up on the security of the military for the uncertainty that laid ahead if I separated.—J.B., Sergeant, 4 years USAF, Loadmaster

Best: Rely on your military training and your network Worst: Civilian jobs offer more than military jobs.—A.T., Capt (ret), 20 years USAF, MSC

Best: It's never too early to begin, and having more time was a good thing. I was able to focus on the retirement process and enjoying my terminal leave rather than launching an all-out job hunt. Worst: employers generally only want folks that can start within about 90 days. Turns out this was not true for me.—K.E., CW4, 20 years USA, Apache Pilot

Best, don't be insecure about IF you can make it in the civilian world. You are a soldier and have gone through so much more than the average American. Don't sell yourself short just because you are unsure of what is on the other side. Don't remain in the military because you like the safety net. When I separated, I had a wife, three kids, two car payments, and a house payment. I survived… Worst, wait for the transition class just before you get out to attend. The was all wrong. I suggest once you decide you are going to make the transition, start looking for the next available class you can get into, and if they have another of the same class before you get out, take it too, as things may have changed or there may be different instructors that have a different vision of what the class is supposed to be like. Repeat as necessary…—J.D. SSgt, 11 USAF, 3 ANG, 1 USAFR, Cyber Systems Operator

[I] did not have a lot of time before I retired after my deployment. [Best] Listen to the staff transitioning briefing. See the local retirement section at MPF, staffed by retirees. Worst was people trying to tell me how to get a better disability rating.—M.M., MSgt (ret), 24.5 USAF, Independent Duty Medical Technician

Best advice: be as patient as you can when job searching. Don't jump at the first offering. I don't know that I received any bad advice, or at least I choose not to remember it.—J.F., MSgt (ret), 20 years USAF, Computer Operations Supervisor

The best advice I received was to start my VA disability compensation application six months prior to exit if possible, and to use my final physical as my VA physical. Those two steps greatly decreased the processing time for my VA disability compensation application. Another critical step was to start working with the transition assistance specialist early, especially on things like your résumé. I thought, how hard could it be to turn over 20 years of military experience into a résumé that civilians would scoop right up? It's hard, very hard. We do so many different things that first you will find that you need more than one résumé. We also speak a different language than civilians. Healthcare fields may be the only career fields that translate directly into civilian healthcare fields. It takes a while to whittle your skills and expertise down to two pages and feel comfortable that it accurately represents your skills and abilities.—J.R., MSgt (ret), 16 years USA, 8 years USAFR

Best – Go to School. Worst – Re-enlist.—D.H., Petty Officer 2nd class, 4 years USN, Court Report/Legal Clerk/Paralegal

The VA physicians telling me "Don't worry, you won't be charged" (and I was) as well as "No talks with our Mental Health or Psychiatric folks regarding PTSD shall ever be disclosed" (and it has been) were the worse; the best I had, none. However, the best of all time has and always shall be "Son, you will find a whole new world out there for you." (My Dad was so right!) My Dad died the week before I left to deploy to Afghanistan.—G.P., Lt Col (ret), 38 yrs 4 months, USAF, CA ANG and USAFR, Medical Service Corps Officer

Best advice – take responsibility for yourself. If you want it – earn it. Nobody gives you anything just because you're a veteran.—J.M., Maj, 26 years USAF, Nurse

Best advice: Attend TAP and take notes. Leverage contracts. Re-tailor your résumé for each job (there is not one-size-fits-all résumé). Keep your résumé short - one page max. No one cares what job you did 20 years ago, so go into detail on the last 10 years, then summarize the rest in a few lines.—Col, 32 years USAF, Aircraft Maintenance and Munitions

Best advice…no one gave that to me. Worst advice, listening to transition programs, and the advice of others on Linked In.—J.G., SSgt, 16 years, USMC/USA, Rifleman/Mortarman/Infantryman

Best – Know your budget ahead of time – expect more expenses (insurance/medical, etc.) and obviously less pay. This will also give you a feel for minimum job income for negotiations etc.—D.Y.

Easiest and hardest part of transition

Everyone's transition is a personal journey. What went right for one person may have gone completely wrong for another one. Good or bad, you reap the rewards. Here's what the service members we interviewed felt was the easiest and toughest part of their transition.

[The easiest part of my transition was the] ability to allow my skills and background to drive my income; freedom to do as I pleased and not have to go where I was ordered to; finding out that the skills I learned in the AF positioned me well to find a good career. The toughest part of my transition was] the loss of [my] AF family; loss of support structure the AF provided; realizing that not every company had the values driven into us as service members; learning to supervise a team that needed a much softer touch than teams managed in the service; knowing I could be unemployed at any time and my family depended on my success.—M.S., TSgt (sep), 11 years USAF, Medical Logistics

The toughest part was the psychological transition over the first couple years. Totally different world out of the Marine Corps. Who's in charge? Did not find a lot of order and organization out here. [Easiest] Growing my beard that I have not shaved off since my retirement! ☺ —W.G., 21 years USMC, Administrative Logistics Management/SIGINT Support

The hardest thing for me was not being part of my group anymore, not being in a spec ops unit, not having that brotherhood, being normal.— W.P., E6(sep), 4 years Navy, 7 years USAR, Diver & Drill Sergeant

It has been easier than I thought it would be, but I fully realize that I walked right into a great job, and that's unusual; and I feel bad for those who were not as fortunate as I was. The toughest part was this; for 27 years I deflected praise, gave all the credit to my people, and shunned the limelight because that's what leaders should do. Also, I was the guy others came to for help. All of a sudden, I was forced to market myself and that was a very tough thing to get used to, as was the fact that I had to ask others for help in one way or another. Very hard to change like that.— K.C., Col (ret), 27 years USA, Military Intelligence Officer

Toughest challenge was wading through the ignorant perceptions of civilian and corporate entities. The easiest was taking that step forward and committing. Everything else is worked on along the way and not that hard with true commitment. —J.G., SSgt, 16 years, USMC/USA, Rifleman/Mortarman/Infantryman

Frankly the easiest thing was getting the job. I was very lucky and it was completely unexpected. I did not apply for it, it was an offer out of the blue. I was locked into this job four months before my transition started. The toughest thing was making the decision to leave my family behind in the States while I complete a year on the job here in Saudi Arabia. I am scoping things out and making arrangements to bring them over next year depending on the security situation. I had to get in the mindset that this is just another deployment. It's very hard to leave them again, but in the end, it's financial security for all of us. —S.D., CW2, 26.5 years, USA, Patton Tanker, Abrams Tanker, Apache Helicopter Repairer, Aircraft Electrical and Environmental Systems Repairer, Apache Helicopter Pilot

[Easiest] I was a Command Sergeant Major so I had instant credibility with the people I work with, both my fellow contractors and uniformed personnel. [Toughest] I am not a Command Sergeant Major

210

anymore, and as a contractor I have no command authority to fix things.—B.O., CMS (ret), 36 years USA & AANG, Senior Engineer Sergeant

The easiest part was that I realized I had the ability to control my future. By taking steps and writing down a five-step Plan of Action, I was able to get hired. The hardest part was realizing that job boards do not result in getting you a job. I sent out over 100 résumés. Only through networking did I get interviews.—R.W., CW4(ret), 23 years 2 weeks USA, Special Operations Pilot

[Easiest] My veteran status gave me a leg up in the job market. I had become very resourceful due to my Air Force training and experience. [Toughest] Leaving your entire social network and way of life for the past four years was difficult. It was difficult assimilating back into civilian life. My experiences were far different than those of nearly everyone I worked with after the military. The first few years back in the civilian workforce are the most difficult. As time went on I accumulated experiences more similar to those around me. It takes some time and you have to work through those first years. It gets better with time.—J.B., Sergeant (sep), 4 years USAF, Loadmaster

Yes, do not think the world owes you anything. Entitlements only keep you a slave to the system of socialistic conditioning. Move past the fear and embarrassment of failure. No one succeeds without failing and the true measure of your characteristic and success is how you get up and keep pushing forward to get what you want and deserve.—J.G., SSgt, 16 years, USMC/USA, Rifleman/Mortarman/Infantryman

211

Good advice

The SMs we interviewed had either gone or were going through transition when we interviewed them. This is the advice they offered to those getting ready to go down the same path.

Always network with everyone you meet. Don't think that the only job has to be an exact match with what you have in the service. Be willing to adapt, as there may be some culture shock when you enter the civilian workforce. Utilize veteran organizations and placement firms to assist you in locating the job. Obtain certifications for a career path you choose. Understand how to translate your military 'language' to civilian terms or corporate terminology. This is key as the interviewer has no understanding of ranks of military acronyms. Apply for every job regardless if it is a stretch or perfect fit for your skills and experience. This allows YOU to choose your path versus taking the first job offered. If you are retiring, realize you may have to start over. This may not mean financially, but may mean taking a position that is not a leadership role. Most companies are reluctant to bring in leadership roles externally although mid-level management roles pay quite well. Never stop looking for something better. Best time to apply for a job is when you already have one. Fight the feeling you must be loyal, as you and only you control your success.—M.S., TSgt, 11 years USAF, Medical Logistics

Keep a positive attitude. This is just a new adventure. Assess your strengths and weaknesses honestly. Don't take no for an answer. Nine times out of 10 there is a way for you to overcome and meet your goal. Use social media in your search. If it weren't for LinkedIn, I wouldn't have this job. Learn to sell yourself. Network, network, network!—S.D., CW2 (ret), 26.5 years AANG/USA/ANG, Patton and Abrams

212

Tanker, Apache Helicopter Repairer, Aircraft Electrical & Environmental Systems Repairer, Apache Helicopter Pilot

Research the locations and companies near the location where you desire employment. Prepare for the jobs you have targeted. Network with individuals with that company. Manage your expectations... avoid thinking you are going to make big money on your first job or it will be for the rest of your life (or another career). Leverage professional associations and network. Draft a résumé for trusted friends in the commercial sector to review. Go to commercial companies and see what they are wearing so you can start building your wardrobe. Use LinkedIn and the web to evaluate companies and develop informal links. Attend open meetings/functions that prospective companies are attending and develop relationships.—A.T., Capt (ret), 20 years USAF, MSC

Use all the resources you can find. P.F., Chief Petty Officer, 23 years USNR, Gunner's Mate

Plan, plan, plan – network, network, network – be a sponge and learn as much as you can. Finally, get good financial advice. Living in the civilian world is not cheap and money runs out fast.—D.R., Col (ret), 31 years USA, Military Intelligence Officer

Get a college degree as early in your career as possible! It shows any perspective employer that you have what it takes to better yourself, work hard, make sacrifices, etc. Earning your degree is also the best way to set you on a path of life-long learning and will make getting a certificate or taking a few extra courses upon separation to prepare you for the career you want. While still serving, accept every opportunity to go to training and leadership schools you can. I have three MOS's, attended every Noncommissioned Officer Course the Army offered, and attended

213

countless other schools that gave me special skill identifiers and qualified me to compete for and earn assignments that most NCOs would never experience.—B.O., CSM (ret), 36 years USA/AANG, Senior Engineer Sergeant

STOP relying on others to leverage you to work for them and pay you pennies on the dollar. Go out there and realize your dream. Get educated and know the difference between fluff and reality.—J.G., SSgt, 16 years, USMC/USA, Rifleman/Mortarman/Infantryman

Pick three things you feel are your talents or skill sets and you want to pursue as a career. Form your plan of action, and do them. Stay connected in your network, join LinkedIn. There are a lot of servicemen out looking for work, and even more are already employed. Don't use your service in the Military or your Combat Skills as a badge in your career. Use your SKILL SET; take action just as you did during the execution of your missions. Recognize that many people you work with already served and were in the place you are now. Ask for help!—R.W. CW4 (ret), 23 years 2 weeks USA, Special Operations Pilot

Consider writing a book about your passion, and publish it online. Join LinkedIn and use it! Seek out the job you want, form a plan of action, and pursue it. You won't get there without a plan. Surround yourself with people in the industry you are passionate about. Seek help from services like this service to help veterans—R.W. CW4 (ret), 23 years 2 weeks USA, Special Operations Pilot

You will have failures; expect them. Know that they are learning experiences. Don't shy away from trying something for fear of failure. In the military, you are trained better than you will be in the future corporate world. The military services train you not to fail. As a result, I initially

214

felt like a failure when I failed in the corporate world. It is difficult to adjust to the fact that the only way you will grow in the corporate world is to accept that failures are steps towards success. Perseverance will take you where you want to go. You will at times fail, but you are not a failure.—J.B., SSgt (sep), 4 years USAF, Loadmaster

Do it on your own terms; do not wait for the military to tell you it's time to go. And please do not stay in the military just because you are afraid of what is on the other side; that's a terrible reason to serve the nation, and it only prolongs the hard work it takes to get out there and make it. The transition will be the toughest and most uncomfortable period of your adult life. However, you have to do it at some point, so embrace it and do it when you want to, where you want to, and under the conditions that are best for you and your family. Don't be afraid; everyone goes through this at some point, and the world is full of people who were one thing for decades and now are something else. It's okay, you will be better for it.—K.C., Col (ret), 27 years USA, Military Intelligence Officer.

Start early (two years out) and prepare a good résumé. If you have [a] higher education degree, put that at the top of your résumé, and if you had really good grades put your GPA on there. List all degrees (if you have a Masters, list your Bachelors also). Get used to talking to strangers – practice this everywhere by simply saying "Hi" as you pass. Exude a positive "can-do" personality. Write down everyone's name that you meet at your target employers, and if you land an interview, immediately send each of them a personalized letter (on good paper and in a matching envelope). Keep it brief and mention something unique that was discussed with each – keep your entire tone positive. The interview begins as you arrive on the property; you never know who's watching you or if someone seemingly not involved in the interview process will have input. (Think about the security guard at the gate, the secretary at the desk, or even the cleaning personnel. Say hello, smile, and treat them all well, because you never know.)—K.E., CW4 (ret), 20 years USA, Apache Pilot

Get or make official copies of all your awards/decorations, medical records, training records/certificates. These come in handy when applying for jobs where experience can substitute for a college degree.—M.M., MSgt (ret), 24.5 years USAF, Independent Duty Medical Technician

Have a Plan A, Plan B, and Plan C at least five years prior to retirement!—K.V., Col (ret), 24 years USAF, Health Service Administrator

In addition to the advice on being as patient as possible, take as much time as you can to prepare: learn how to interview, and have your résumé professionally prepared, if you can. If not, have it reviewed by people you trust. Dress well for your interview, even if the job itself doesn't require it. Do your best to remain positive; it's a difficult employment climate now.— J.F., MSgt (ret), 20 years USAF, Computer Operations Supervisor

Don't worry, but do plan. Don't let the transition sneak up on you. Expect the unexpected, but don't expect that you will change the way you think and proceed with your work the day you put on a suit. The longer you spend in the military, expect it to take 1/3 of that same time to adjust your style to the environment and culture of the civilian workforce. We always focus on being civilian employment-ready with our education and résumés, but we are not focusing any effort in preparing service members for the leadership, communication, and other style changes that may need to be addressed as the service member makes this transition. Not all need this help, but for those who served much or all their adult life in highly tactical environments, where the culture of the work environment is a complete 180 of the culture in the civilian workplace, this topic is highly

216

underserved.—J.R., MSgt (ret), 23 years USA, USAFR, Army Combat Medic/Aerospace Medical Technician

This [advice] depends on the person who is receiving the advice. A person like me – enlisted at the end of a four-year hitch ... go to school is what I would advise. An enlisted Navy pipe-fitter would perhaps be better served in joining a pipe-fitter union and going through their apprenticeship program; an officer with a Liberal Arts degree from some University at the end of his required time might try graduate school; enlisted at the end of 20 years would need something else, as would a service academy grad. I guess my suggestion is for the service member to plan before leaving the service on what they would like to do upon leaving, so they can step into the activity quickly. There is really no "one size fits all" advice for future transitioning service members. Each has their own challenges and obstacles. It is important for the new civilian to have a goal and work towards that goal, with the understanding the need to be flexible and adjust the goal as they progress.—D.H., Petty Officer 2nd Class, 4 years Navy, Court Report/Legal Clerk/Paralegal

Start planning well in advance of retirement for it; five years or more, to decide where you want to root yourself, what career field you desire, or schooling necessary to sustain yourself and what you want to be till and when you retire.—G.P., Lt Col (ret), 38 years 4 months USAFR, Medical Service Corps Officer

Search your soul, and ensure no regrets before leaving the service. You will know in your heart that it is time and no one will be able to talk you out of it. Talk with family and close friends to describe your plan and let them help refine it. For those VSI [very seriously injured], medical care can be and [is] often delivered from multiple sources, which can be confusing, frustrating and unfamiliar. Be strong and maintain

217

professionalism with those trying to get help. If you feel you cannot do that, then choose a family member or close friend to keep you calm. Stress of being upset will not do anyone any good and will not assist in your successful transition or healing.—M.G., Lt Col (ret), 3.5 years USAR, 22 years USAFR, Medical Service Corps Officer

Make sure that you plan and save for transition. You need to be mentally prepared also; the military takes very good care of you and does a lot of things for you that you take for granted.—W.H., SSgt, 11 ½ years USAF, Aerospace Medical Journeyman

Since being in the civilian world, I have had the opportunity to interview several veterans for jobs in my ER. Some believe that they are owed a job just because they are veterans or because they were deployed. I am also a police officer, and have had veterans tell me that I shouldn't arrest them after breaking the law because they were deployed and they fought for my rights. As a veteran, you should be held to a higher standard than the civilian. You have had the training—use it!—J.M., Maj (ret), 26 years USAF, Nurse

Don't accept the first job that comes along if it's not really what you want to do or where you want to be. I turned [down] a high profile, well-paying job in Louisiana after seeing the location. The facility was great, the job was superb, but Lake Charles sucked... really sucked. Practice interviewing – a lot. Once you think you've mastered it, you are about halfway there... Once offered a salary figure, ask for 10 percent more. No one will laugh at you; the most they'll do is say no, that they made a firm deal and final offer. But 10 percent is about what a business expects for a recruit to counter with, and most will say yes. Thus, in about five seconds you already made an extra $7,000-12,000 a year! Colonels sell themselves short—your post-AF starting income should be close to or *exceed six figures. General Officers overestimate their worth and often find themselves doing "independent consulting." They need to touch up their technical skills and expect salaries closer to those [of] retiring Chiefs and Colonels unless they were in program management or were politically well-connected to corporate executives.—Col, 32 years USAF, Aircraft Maintenance and Munitions*

Set goals, do not expect to get what you want overnight, work smart; network, network, network. Get involved in volunteer work and help your fellow veterans, take courses, use on-line information to your advantage… maintain absolute integrity in all you do, helping others along the way. Be positive, read inspirational books, surround yourself with vibrant, positive, professional, and generous people who know how to give back as well as receive.—W.G., 21 years USMC, Administrative Logistics Management/SIGINT Support

We all have different reasons for leaving the military. It's an important chapter in your life; be prepared to share it with others, especially those who want to follow in your footsteps and enter the military.

Your combat reflexes that you developed in country (you know, ducking when you hear a loud BANG) are not PTSD… that shit SAVED YOUR LIFE in combat, and you are still conditioned to respond that way. It's not a big deal, and it's nothing to be embarrassed about! E.C., Captain, US Army Infantry, 1997-2008, Organization: HHC, 1-160 IN, 40th Infantry Div, California Army National Guard, Commander, HHC, 1-160 IN, Santa Ana, deployed to Kosovo as part of KFOR 6A-6B 2004-2006.

Notes:

_____

_____

_____

_____

_____

_____

_____

_____

_____

_____

_____

_____

_____

_____

Notes:

_____

_____

_____

_____

_____

_____

_____

_____

_____

_____

_____

_____

_____

_____

_____

12. Resources

Never forget the three powerful resources you always have available to you: love, prayer, and forgiveness.—H. Jackson Brown, author, *Life's Little Instruction Book.*

What's Next?

Many service members have an internal bucket list in the back of their heads, consisting of things they've always wanted to do but have never really thought much about. The opportunities are endless, but your time and resources are not. Hopefully this book will not only give you ideas on your next mission, but also how to *Charlie Mike*, continue the mission, by going forward.

Our lives are not about time management, but priority management. That means making a list of those things that interest you, prioritizing those items that seem like your best fit for your life, and then taking action on those ideas. You can't steer a parked car, so it's a matter of taking stock, finding your new mission, and pressing on.

Organizations and Web Sites to Help

The list of potential resources you can tap for your next adventure is very long and constantly growing, making it impossible to be all inclusive. But the list below at least gets you started with your transition research. Some of these resources fit into multiple categories, but we've done our best to find the best fit, to make it easier for you to peruse.

223

Educational resources

When it comes to educational resources, consider that in some cases you can learn more on your own than through other sources. Given that some sources of education are between 5-7 years behind the marketplace with certain skills and technologies, it might behoove you to search out up-to-date sources of skills. Arguably, not all "old timer" skill sets, like computer programming languages such as COBOL or FORTRAN, are obsolete, but are used less than other technologies. Research all appropriate avenues for learning new skills.

Federal Student Aid	studentaid.ed.gov
GI Bill	benefits.va.gov/gibill
Military Connection	militaryconnection.com/education
Troops to Teachers	troopstoteachers.net
LinkedIn	veterans.linkedin.com
Yellow Ribbon Program	newgibill.org/yellow-ribbon-program

Employment

You can check out any number of web sites for employment.

American Corporate Partners	acp-usa.org
American Heroes at Work	americasheroesatwork.gov

American Job Center	jobcenter.usa.gov
Americorps	nationalservice.gov/programs/americorps
Americorps State and National	" "
Americorps VISTA	" "
Americorps NCCC - Femacorps	" "
Army Civilian Service	armycivilianservice.com
Army COOL	cool.army.mil
Bradley Morris, Inc	bradley-morris.com
Career One Stop	careeronestop.org
Career Scope	benefits.va.gov/gibill/careerscope.asp
Corporate Gray	corporategray.com
DoD Transition Assistance Program (DoDTAP)	https://www.dmdc.osd.mil/tgps/
E2I	warriorcare.dodlive.mil/wounded-warrior-resources/e2i/
FedBizOpps	fbo.gov
Feds Hire Vets	fedshirevets.gov/
Federal Motor Carrier Safety Administration	fmcsa.dot.gov (See Registration > Commercial Drivers License > Military)

Gallant Few	gallantfew.org
Gold Card	dol.gov/vets/goldcard.html
Hire Our Heroes	hireourheroes.org
Hire Heroes USA	hireheroesusa.org
My Career @ VA	mycareeratva.va.gov
My Next Move	mynextmove.org/vets
	mynextmove.org/explore/lp
NAFJOBS	nafjobs.org
Navy COOL	cool.navy.mil/One
Stop Career Center	servicelocator.org
Operation Warfighter	warriorcare.mil
Playsmint	playsmint.com
REALifelines	dol.gov/vets/programs/REAL-life/
VA for Vets	vaforvets.va.gov
Vets Employment Program Office	dm.usda.gov/employ/vepo
Vocational Rehab	benefits.va.gov/vocrehab/index.asp
US Small Business Administration	sba.gov
USAJOBS	usajobs.gov

Entrepreneurship and startups

When it comes entrepreneurship, start-ups, business, and economics, some will say there are no differences between the terms. Ask any entrepreneur, and they'll beg to differ. While each term has their common core of topics and terms, they all have enough differences to warrant knowing why each is different.

Below is a list of websites of information. Don't forget to look at the footers or the site maps to see what other links to other resources are available.

SCORE	score.org/
Veteran Entrepreneurial Portal	va.gov/osdbu/entrepreneur/index.asp
Americas Fund	americasfund.org
Brave-Aid Inc	braveaid.org
Evan Ashcraft Foundation	evanashcraft.org
EBV National Program	ebv.vets.syr.edu
Healing Heroes	healingheroes.org
Heartbeat for Warriors (WA state)	heartbeatforwarriors.org
Housing Grants for Disabled veterans	benefits.va.gov/homeloans/adapted housing.asp
Fannie Mae Military Forbearance Option	knowyouroptions.com/find-resources/government-programs/military-options

Impact A Hero	impactplayer.org
Independence Fund	independencefund.org
Lead the Way Fund (Army Ranger)	leadthewayfund.org
Military Saves	militarysaves.org
On Behalf	onbehalf.org
Operation Family Fund	operationfamilyfund.org
Operation Once in a Lifetime	operationonceinalifetime.com
Operation One Voice	operationonevoice.org
Pennsylvania Wounded Warriors	pawoundedwarriors.org
Patriot Boot Camp	http://www.patriotbootcamp.org
Rebuild Hope	rebuildhope.org
Red Circle Foundation (Special Ops)	redcirclefoundation.org
Salute America's Heroes	saluteheroes.org
Salute, Inc	saluteinc.org
Special Operations Warrior Foundation	specialops.org
TAMCO Foundation	tamcofoundation.org
The General's Kids	thegeneralkids.org

The Home Front Cares (CO)	thehomefrontcares.org
Reserveaid	reserveaid.org
USA Cares	usacares.org

Health

After Deployment	afterdeployment.org
Army Warrior Transition Command	wtc.army.mil
AF Wounded Warrior Program	woundedwarrior.af.mil
Anxiety and Depression Association of America	adaa.org
Coaching into Care	mirecc.va.gov/coaching/index.asp
Defense Centers of Health	dcoe.mil
Defense and Veteran's Brain Injury Center	dvbic.dcoe.mil
Deployment Health Clinical Center	pdhealth.mil/main.asp
Dstressline	dstressline.com
Fairways for Warriors	fairwaysforwarriors.org
Grace After Fire	graceafterfire.org
Give an Hour	giveanhour.org
Helios Warrior	helioswarrior.org

Kristin Brooks Hope Center	1 800 SUICIDE, hopeline.com
Lone Survivor Foundation	lonesurvivorfoundation.org
The Merritt Center	merrittcenter.org
Military Pathways	militarymentalhealth.org
Marine Wounded Warrior Regiment	woundedwarriorregiment.org
Mental Health America	mentalhealthamerica.net
Military Health System	health.mil
MyHealtheVet	myheatlh.va.gov
National Center for PTSD	ptsd.va.gov/public/index.asp
National Center for Telehealth and Technology	t2health.dcoe.mil
National Intrepid Center of Excellence	nicoe.capmed.mil
Navy Wounded Warrior - Safe Harbor	safeharbor.navylive.dodlive.mil
Naval Center Combat and Operational Stress Control (NCCOSC)	med.navy.mil/sites/nmcsd/nccosc
Real Warriors	realwarriors.net
Returning Veteran's Project	returningveterans.org
The Soldier's Project	thesolidersproject.org
SHARE Military Initiative (Shepherd Center)	shepherd.org/patient-programs/care-for-us-service-members
Soldier's Heart	solidersheart.net

Strategic Outreach to Families of All Reservists (SOFAR)	sofarusa.org
Vet Center	vetcenter.va.gov
Veterans' Families United Foundation	veteransfamiliesunited.org
Vets2Vets 1-877-VET2VET	veteranscall.us
Vets To Vets United	vetstovetsunited.org
Vets 4 Warriors	vets4warriors.com
War Related Illness and Injury Study Center	warrelatedillness.va.gov

Women's veterans groups

During the 1980s, women comprised about eight percent of the military; today, women represent about 14 percent of those in the service. While both men and women suffer from similar issues after leaving the service, there are differences. Organizations that specifically aid women veterans include:

Women's Veteran Health	womenshealth.va.gov
American Women Veterans	americanwomenveterans.org/home/
Grace After Fire	graceafterfire.org
Service Women's Action Network	servicewomen.org
Women Veterans Rock	womenvetsrock.org

Operation Reinvent	operationreinvent.org

General resources

You can find additional and various resources below.

Web sites

American Campaign	americancampaign.org
American Freedom Foundation	americanfreedomfoundation.com
American Legion	legion.org
Association of Defense Communities	defensecommunities.org/tag/civilia n-transition/#
Blind Veterans Association	bva.org
Disabled American Veterans	dav.org
Ebenefits	ebenefits.va.gov
Got Your 6	gotyour6.org
Hope for the Warrior	hopeforthewarriors.org
Impact a Hero	impactplayer.org
Iraq and Afghanistan Veterans of America	iava.org
Military Friendly	militaryfriendly.com

Military Officers Association of America	moaa.org
Military OneSource	militaryonesource.mil
	military.com
National Association of American veterans	naavets.org
National Military Family Association	militaryfamily.org
National Resource Directory	https://www.nrd.gov/
Operation Homefront	operationhomefront.net
Operation Once in a Lifetime	operationonceinalifetime.com
Operation Second Chance	operationsecondchance.org
Operation We Are Here	operationwearehere.com
Raider Project	raiderproject.org
Social Innovation Fund	nationalservice.gov/programs/social-innovation-fund
SOCOM Care Coalition	socom.mil/Care%20Coalition/Default.aspx
State Military and Veterans Site	statelocalgov.net/50states-military-veterans.cfm
U.S. Vets	usvetsinc.org
Veteran Families United Foundation	veteranfamiliesunited.org

Vets First	vetsfirst.org
Veterans of Foreign War (VFW)	vfw.org
Yellow Ribbon Program	yellowribbon.mil

Multi-service resources

Asset Building Network	assetbuildingnetwork.org
Hope for the Warriors	hopeforthewarriors.org
Interfaith Community Services (Oceanside and Escondido CA)	interfaithservices.org
Lutheran Services (Carolinas)	lscarolinas.net
Madison Street Veterans (Phoenix, AZ)	madisonstreetveterans.org
Military Missions In Action (MMIA)	militarymissionsinaction.org
Rocky Mountain Human Services – Military/Veteran Programs (CO and So. WY)	rmhumanservices.org/program/military-veteran-programs
Vetfriends	vetfriends.com

Services

America's Vet Dog	vetdogs.org
Armed Forces Foundation	armedforcesfoundation.org

Building for America's Bravest	ourbravest.org/
Building Homes for Heroes	buildinghomesforheroes.com
Disabled Veteran Committee on Housing	dvchvets.org/
Helping A Hero	helpingahearo.org
Homeowners Assistance Program	hap.usace.army.mil
Home Depot Foundation	homedepotfoundation.org
Jared Allen Foundation	jaredallen69inc.com
Lift For A Vet	iuec5.com/lift_for_a_vet.aspx
Minnesota Assistance Council for veterans	http://www.mac-v.org
Operation Finally Home	http://operationfinallyhome.org
Operation Forever Free	http://www.operatioinforeverfree.org
Purple Heart Homes	purplehearthomesusa.org
Quality of Life Foundation	qolfoundation.org
Rebuild Together	rebuildtogether.org
Specialty Adapted Housing Agents	benefits.va.gov/homeloans/contact_agents.asp
Warrior Gateway	warriorgateway.org
Wounded Warriors in Action	wwiaf.org/

Studies

Research Match	https://www.researchmatch.org
VA Cooperative Study Program	http://www.research.va.gov/programs/csp/studies.cfm
VA Public Health Studies	publichealth.va.gov/exposures/research-studies.asp
Veteran Study Program	http://veteranstudy.blogspot.com

Transition resources

Air Compassion for Veteran	aircompassionforveterans.org
Alpha Omega	alphaomegaveterans.org
Arizona Heroes to Hometowns	azheroestohometowns.org
Final Salute, Inc	finalsaluteinc.org
In Transition	intransition.dcoe.mil/
Lone Star Veterans Association	lonestarveterans.org
Marine for Life	marineforlife.org
Military Warriors Support Foundation	militarywarriors.org
TeamUp	vacteamup.org/

Transition Assistance Online (TAOnline)	taonline.com
Vet List	houstonveterans.org
Veterati	veterati.com
Veterans Rebuilding Life	veteransrebuildinglife.org

Volunteer/Nonprofit

Keep in mind that all of these places in each category of this list are potential places to volunteer at.

American Red Cross	redcross.org
Blue Star Family	bluestarfam.org
Bob Woodruff Foundation	bobwoodrufffoundation.org/
Give an Hour	giveanhour.org/
Goodwill	goodwill.org/
Habitat for Humanity	habitat.org/
Joining Forces	whitehouse.gov/joiningforces
Lotsa Helping Hands	lotsahelpinghands.com
Matthew Freeman Project	freemanproject.org

Military Education Coalition	militarychild.org/
Operation Promise for Service Members	operationpromiseforservicemembers.com
Pat Tillman Foundation	pattillmanfoundation.org
Peace Corps	peacecorps.gov
Points of Light	pointsoflight.org/
Seniorcorps	nationalservice.gov/programs/senior-corps
Sierra Club	sierraclub.org
Story Corps	storycorps.org
Student veterans of America	studentveterans.org
Tragedy Assistance Program for Survivors	taps.org
Teach for America	teachforamerica.org
Team Red, White and Blue	teamrwb.org
Team Rubicon	teamrubiconusa.org
The 6th Branch	the6thbranch.org
The Mission Continues	missioncontinues.org
USO	uso.org

Veteran Artist Program	veteranartistprogram.org
Veterans in Film and Television	vftla.org
Volunteers for America	voa.org

Books and Magazines:

Returning Wars' Wounded, Injured, and Ill edited by Nathan D. Ainspan and Walter E. Penk.

Veterans Voices: Remarkable Stories of Heroism, Sacrifice, and Honor by Robert H. Miller and Andrew Wakeford

The Veteran's Survival Guide: How to File and Collect on VA Claims, Second Edition by John D. Roche

Women Vietnam Veterans: Our Untold Stories by Donna A. Lowery

See Me for Who I Am: Student Veterans' Stories of War and Coming Home by David Chrisinger

Veterans' Guide to One Million in the Bank by Michael L.F. Slavin

The Military to Civilian Transition Guide by Carl S. Savino and Ronald L. Krannich, PhD.

G.I. Job (monthly magazine)

Stars and Stripes Transition Magazine (quarterly magazine)

Veteran's Education Guide (www.vetsguide.com)

Business trainers do an exercise where they ask their students to write letters to themselves projecting one year into the future what they hope to accomplish. The company then mails the letter after the year is up, so people can reflect on what they accomplished with what they dreamt of. You can try doing this yourself.

You, Veteran: looking backward to look forward. Whether you served a few years or until you retired after decades of service, you're closing out one chapter of your life. As you contemplate your next chapter, we hope this book will give you morsels of knowledge to assist you in developing a game plan. The historical content will give you the chance to look back to see where we've come from—and the understanding that you stand on the shoulders of other veterans who have come before you. We wanted to help you see what they have done with their service, and with their lives after their service. We also hope that through this look back at American veteran history, combined with the look forward information that we've provided, you'll find your next adventure in life

As you have learned from the veterans in this book, the road is not straight and flat. It is often curved, hilly, and on occasion hits a dead-end. No matter, don't give up! If you fall, get back up and continue your adventure. If you need help, call out to other veterans for a helping hand. And in kind, be there for others that may also need a hand. At the end of the day, the path forged and the story told will be yours. How you vision the ending and how it truly ends is solely determined by you. We hope this book provides you tools and resources to assist you in making your transition from Warrior to Patriot Citizen an enormous success.

The sky really is the limit... if you're prepared.

Notes:

_____

_____

_____

_____

_____

_____

_____

_____

_____

_____

_____

_____

_____

_____

Notes:

Appendix. Our National Startup
and Veteran Legislation

"Build me a son, O Lord, who will be strong enough to know when he is weak, and brave enough to face himself when he is afraid, one who will be proud and unbending in honest defeat, and humble and gentle in victory." – General Douglas MacArthur

American veterans have had their ups and downs when it comes to their post-military careers. The current Veterans Administration (VA) can trace its roots back to 1636, when the Pilgrims of Plymouth Colony were at war with the Pequot Indians. The Pilgrims of the era enacted a law that committed them to support soldiers disabled while defending the colony.[48]

In this appendix, we'll provide a brief list of American conflicts and wars,[49] but more importantly, we'll share some context about those wars and then look at veteran life stories and associated legislative actions, asking questions like: How were veterans treated by American society and government via legislation? After their service, how did some veterans transition to the civilian world and move on with their lives?

National Military Snapshot. America didn't have much of a professional military until the late 1800s and early 1900s. A number of:

---

[48] helpdesk.vetsfirst.org in the *veterans Guide to VA Benefits.*
[49] wikipedia.org; See *List of conflicts in the United States*

...soldiers and legislators, including Washington, Knox, Hamilton and John Adams, desiring to eliminate America's wartime reliance on foreign engineers and artillerists, urged the creation of an institution devoted to the arts and sciences of warfare. President Thomas Jefferson signed legislation establishing the United States Military Academy in 1802. He took this action after ensuring that those attending the Academy would be representative of a democratic society.[50]

In most cases, a military conflict required a new military buildup and training of military conscripts and called-up citizens for the cause. Andrew Carnegie wrote in his 1886 book *Triumphant Democracy* about the approach to our national military:

In military and naval power the Republic is at once the weakest and the strongest of the nations. Her regular army consists of 25,000 men scattered all over the continent in companies of fifty or a hundred. Her navy, thank God! is as nothing. But twenty years ago, as at the blast of a trumpet, she called into action two millions of armed men, and floated six hundred and twenty-six warships. Even the vaunted legions of Xerxes, and the hordes of Attila and Timour were exceeded in numbers by the citizen soldiers who took up arms in 1861 to defend the unity of the nation, and who, when the task was done, laid them quietly down, and returned to the avocations of peace.[51]

Carnegie goes on further to comment regarding our military buildup and subsequent RIF (Reduction in Force) of the military and the American citizen's ideals:

---

[50] At http://www.usma.edu; See *A Brief History of West Point.*
[51] *Triumphant Democracy* by Andrew Carnegie, pp. 5-6

As Macaulay says of the soldiers of the Commonwealth: "In a few months there remained not a trace indicating that the most formidable army in the world had just been absorbed into the mass of the community." And the character of the Republic's soldiers, too, recalls his account of this Republic's army of Cromwell's. "Royalist themselves confessed that, in every department of honest industry, the discarded warriors prospered beyond other men, that none was charged with any theft or robbery, that none was heard to ask for alms, and that if a baker, a mason, or a waggoner attracted notice by his diligence and sobriety, he was in all probability one of Oliver's old soldiers." This was when the parent land was free from hereditary rulers and under the invigorating influence of republican institutions. Thus do citizens fight on one side of the Atlantic as on the other, and, grander far, thus return to the pursuits of peace. Not for throne, for king, or for privileged class, but for Country, *for a country which gives to the humblest every privilege accorded to the greatest.*[52]

Today's returning veterans aren't much different from those who have gone before us, before or after military service. We carry on. It's from this proud and humble foundation and tradition that today's veterans continue in likewise honorable fashion after leaving the service. That "mission first" mentality translates from a service member's work in the military, with bombs and bullets, to a veteran's work in the marketplace with production and profit.

Veteran Legislation. By no means are the legislative acts listed below complete or comprehensive; but they do provide a glimpse of the legislation of the various time periods to show Americans viewed our veterans and their service, and the struggles and conflicts endured to compensate veterans and their families for their sacrifices. We do

---

[52]Carnegie, pp. 5-6

not attempt to rank or catalog all the legislation enacted, but try to provide a glimpse into what was discussed and passed. As with any legislation, what and when veterans really needed help may not have been what was actually passed by our representatives. Many factors are involved. In most cases, a price tag and a time frame were attached to specific legislation—and therein lies the rub.

1700s: Startup Nation and Revolution

During the first two-thirds of the 1700s, American considered themselves British subjects. While American colonial businessmen engaged in transatlantic commerce during the first half of the eighteenth century nearly "all extolled the mutual benefits of the imperial relationship and argued that the Americans were happy to be a part of the British empire. "[53]

Eleven years passed between Britain's first attempt to tax the colonists and the Declaration of Independence. The struggle and war had gone on for 15 months before the Continental Congress declared independence, "not for American independence, but to be reunited with Great Britain on America's terms."[54] Benjamin Franklin spoke somewhat prophetically of the relationship between American colonists and Britain: a "wise and good Mother" ... would loosen her grip on her maturing offspring, lest tight restraints "distress...the children" and "weaken...the whole family."[55]

The increasingly prevalent British attitudes toward the colonies, based primarily on British political decisions of the mid-1700s, saw America only as a source of income and raw materials for England, staffed by social dregs and criminals rather than the thriving new

---

[53] *Independence* by John Ferling, p. 12
[54] *Ibid,* p. x
[55] *Ibid,* p. 12

economy bursting with opportunity that it was. The colonists had fled class-ridden conformity or outright tyranny and started fresh in a new land, creating a culture of those willing to dare, to take risks—not just to be innovative, but inventive, putting their innovations to good use on a daily basis. Colonialists became more than inventors, they became entrepreneurs.[56] America's largest city, Philadelphia, had over 40,000 inhabitants—making it more populous than England's second largest city, Bristol.[57]

Up until the mid-1700s, things went well for the Americans. Then the British began their economic policies of taxation without representation and other restrictive legislations to help fund their wars and wrest economic control from the soon-to-be-rebellious colonists' hands. They could not have prepared us better for revolution if they had deliberately tried.

The British attempt to control the Americans came through taxes to aggrandize funds for British war debts.[58] During the mid-1700s, the ever-increasing economic restrictions of the Molasses (1733), Sugar (1764), Stamp (1765), Townshend (1767), and Tea (1773) Acts enacted by the British increasingly provided fuel for the American Revolution, stoking American distrust of the British government's legislative actions. Frustration was being collected and stacked like cordwood on a bonfire; but the spark of the American Revolutionary war was long in coming, occurring only when, during the Battle of Lexington and Concord, "the shot heard 'round the world" startled us into action.

Over a decade of fighting concluded with American independence from the British Empire. The end of the American Revolution not only changed how our nation was governed, but also brought a new and different view of both economics and entrepreneurship to the young

---

[56] *They Made America* by Harold Evans, pp. 10-11
[57] *Ibid*, p. 1.
[58] *How Capitalism Saved America,* by Thomas DiLorenzo, pp. 67-78.

new American nation: individualistic, self-determining, competitive, and anti-aristocrat.[59]

This new American attitude was now all about earned success, not selected, bought, given, or inherited titles. It was about self-reliance for every American and his family, and this attitude was strong among the veterans.

Struggles of a New Nation, Veterans, Families, and Communities. As with all conflicts and wars, those who fought during the Revolution paid a price to earn their freedom and the freedom of their fellow citizens. The signors of the Declaration risked and paid dearly for putting their signature on the document. One such example is Thomas Nelson:

> *Thomas Nelson, signer of Virginia, was at the front in command of the Virginia military forces. With British General Charles Cornwallis in Yorktown, fire from 70 heavy American guns began to destroy Yorktown piece by piece. Lord Cornwallis and his staff moved their headquarters into Nelson's palatial home. While American cannonballs were making a shambles of the town, the house of Governor Nelson remained untouched. Nelson turned in rage to the American gunners and asked, "Why do you spare my home?" They replied, "Sir, out of respect to you." Nelson cried, "Give me the cannon!" and fired on his magnificent home himself, smashing it to bits. But Nelson's sacrifice was not quite over. He had raised $2 million for the Revolutionary cause by pledging his own estates. When the loans came due, a newer peacetime Congress refused to honor them, and Nelson's property was forfeited. He was never reimbursed. He died, impoverished, a few years later at the age of 50.[60]*

---

[59] *The First Tycoon: Life of Cornelius Vanderbilt,* by T. J. Stiles, pp. 41, 95.

[60] rushlimbaugh.com; See *My Father's Speech.*

The rest of the signors were about equally ruined. They all became the subjects of manhunts and were driven from their homes. Nine died of wounds or hardships during the war; five were captured and imprisoned, and in each case with brutal treatment. Several lost wives, sons or entire families. John Hart of Trenton, New Jersey, lost all of his 13 children. Abraham Clark's two sons served in the officer corps in the Revolutionary Army. Taken captive, they were imprisoned in the infamous British prison hulk[61] afloat in New York harbor, where 11,000 American captives died. Clark's sons were treated with more brutality than the other Americans, because of who their father was. Toward the end of the war, the British offered him his sons' lives if he would recant and come out for the King and Parliament. With anguish and despair, he replied, "No!"

Not one American defected or went back on his pledged word. Their honor, the principles they stood for, and the nation they sacrificed so much to create is still intact.

Veteran life stories.

- **Alexander Hamilton** (1755–1804) was a political scientist, government official, journalist, military leader, economist, and lawyer. He served under Washington, and later because our first Secretary of Treasury under Washington's presidency. After a election dispute with Aaron Burr, Burr challenged Hamilton to a duel in which Hamilton was mortally wounded.
- **Paul Revere** (1735-1818) was one of five riders to for inform us the British were coming, along with William Dawes, Samuel Prescott, Israel Bissell, and a woman, Sybil Ludington.[62] Revere was an artisan who "augmented his income by becoming an engraver and dentist, was by the 1760s a master goldsmith,

---

[61] wikipedia.org See *List of British prison hulks.*
[62] constitutionfacts.com See *Voices of the Revolution: The Five Riders.*

faring well in a city that was struggling economically, squeezed by British tax policies. Following the war, Revere continued to build on his reputation as a master craftsman and industrialist. He learned to roll copper and opened the country's first copper-rolling mill. In addition, he operated a hardware store and later a foundry."[63]

- **Peter Mackintosh** (1757-1846) served as an apprentice artificer contributing to the war efforts, and witnessed the three hours of the dumping of 45 tons of tea during the Boston Tea Party. He later served a stint as a private in an artillery regiment. In later years, Peter remained active in the Massachusetts Charitable Mechanic Association and as an artificer/blacksmith.[64]

1800s Wars, Conflicts, and Legislation

War of 1812, 1812-1815. The U.S. declared war on Britain in June 1812, in what was essentially a continuation of the American War of Independence. While both the causes and consequences of the war are up for debate, the foundational issue of its success or failure is rarely debated. America was too young and immature as a nation, its government too feeble and inexperienced, which caused considerable bungling and mismanagement during and after the war.[65]

After the war, the United States of America was a singular term, not a plural. If nothing else, the war renewed and reinstated the national feeling and character the Revolution had given us, which had lessened over time. The war was part of a search for a national identity that had "forged a nation."[66]

---

[63] biography.com See *Paul Revere Biography*.

[64] *Don't Tread On Me* by Joseph Bauman, Chapter 1 of the Kindle edition.

[65] *The War of 1812: A Forgotten Conflict, Bicentennial Edition* by Donald Hickey, p. 2

[66] *1812: The War That Forged a Nation* by Walter R. Borneman, pp. 303-304.

Veteran life stories.

- **Davy Crockett** (1786-1836) was a frontiersman who fought in the War of 1812, and afterwards served both as a state representative and U.S. Congressman. Becoming disillusioned with politics after an election defeat, he joined the fight in the Texas War of Independence and died at the Alamo.[67]

- **Andrew Jackson** (1767-1845) joined the local militia at age 13 after his brother died during the Revolutionary War, serving as a courier. Later he became a lawyer and wealthy land owner; and even though lacked significant military experience, he was appointed a major general in the Tennessee militia in 1802 at the age of 35. His military successes during the War of 1812 gave rise to his political career, during which he served as a U.S. Congressman and two terms as President of the U.S.[68]

Mexican–American War, 1846-1848. The U.S. Army was unprepared for this war. While Congress had authorized a strength of 8,613 men and officers, the actual number of soldiers in uniform at the time was fewer than 5,500.[69]

Because the US was still a "startup nation," between its citizens and the militia and military, there was a second wave of volunteers in 1847 to serve for the period of the war—26,922 regular military service members, in contrast with the 73,260 volunteers[70] from 24 states that sent volunteers. Poor sanitation contributed to the spread of illness, with volunteers—who were less disciplined in their sanitary practices than regular troops—suffering 11,550 deaths. This contrasts with the approximately 1,733 regular service members who were killed in action or died of battle wounds (war casualties estimates vary).[71]

---

[67] biography.com See *Davey Crockett.*
[68] biography.com; See *Andrew Jackson.*
[69] pbs.org See *The American Army in the Mexican War: An Overview.*
[70] *Ibid.*
[71] Department of VA, Office of Public Affairs, See *America's Wars.*

What about the veterans of this war?

When the Civil War came in 1861, many of the most noteworthy generals on both sides had profited from their battle experience in the Mexican-American War, including Confederate Generals Robert E. Lee, Thomas ("Stonewall") Jackson, James Longstreet, George Pickett, Albert Sidney Johnston, Lewis Armistead, and P.G.T. Beauregard, as well as Union Generals Ulysses S. Grant (who later called the Mexican War "one of the most unjust ever waged by a stronger against a weaker nation"), George Gordon Meade, George H. Thomas, and Joseph Hooker.[72]

President Polk's decision to enter the war filled out the present boundaries of the continental United States, literally enlarging the nation from "sea to shining sea."

Veteran life stories.

• **Christopher "Kit" Carson** (1809-1868) was an explorer, military leader, and folk hero. At 16, he became a trapper and a mountain man in the West. In 1842, Carson met John C. Frémont, an officer with the United States Topographical Corps, who hired Carson to join him as a guide. Carson was caught in the Mexican War when Frémont's mission changed to a military one. After the war, Carson was appointed a Ute and Apache Indian agent. During the Civil War, Carson led New Mexico volunteers on the Union side. Carson later returned to New Mexico, where he lived out the rest of his life as a rancher.[73]

• **Edgar Allan Poe** (1809-1849) was reared by his adoptive father, wealthy tobacco merchant John Allan, to be a businessman and Virginia gentleman. Poe had little interest in business, and had

---

[72] britannica.com See *Mexican-American War.*
[73] biography.com See Kit Carson

dreams of being a writer. He attended college, but became debt-ridden. Poe enlisted in the army and later, with help from his father, received an appointment to West Point Military Academy. Because of a family fight with Allan, Poe was thrown out. He ultimately became an American writer, editor, and literary critic.[74]

- **David Farragut** (1801-1870) was a career military officer of the U.S. Navy, and is remembered in U.S. Navy tradition for his order at the Battle of Mobile Bay (in which he was victorious): "Damn the torpedoes, full steam ahead.". Farragut remained on active duty for the rest of his life.[75]
- **Ulysses S. Grant** (1822-1885) graduated from West Point in 1843, later becoming Commanding General of the Union Army during the Civil War, and 18th President of the U.S.

American Civil War, 1861-1865. Historian Larry Schweikart writes concerning the Civil War soldiers:

War taught many enlisted men and officers important new skills. Building railroads, bridges, and other constructions turned many soldiers into engineers; the demands of communications introduced many others to Morse Code and the telegraph; keeping the army supplied taught thousands of men teamster skills ... One Chicago print shop, for example, employed 47 former soldiers. ... Nothing enhanced sales like spreading the word that the proprietor was a veteran.[76]

As with most military jobs, the skills needed to perform them required learning new or different skills and habits that service members may not have been accustomed to, or improving from basic to advanced skills or habits compared with what they were working

---

[74] poemuseum.org See *Poe's Life*.
[75] civilwar.org See *David G. Farragut*
[76] *A Patriot's History of the United States* by Larry Schweikart & Michael Allen, p. 358.

with at home. With most veterans, anything learned from the military could be used in the marketplace as a newly minted civilian and now a military veteran.

The U.S. military mustered out about 800,000 soldiers after the Civil War, and slashed the Navy from 700 ships down to fewer than 250. A total of 3.2 million people served during the Civil War, 2.2 million for the Union and 1 million on the Confederacy, with over 140,000 and 74,000 battle deaths for their respective sides.[77] About 17 percent of the American population served during the Civil War.[78]

Since the Civil War was fought on American soil, the devastation took years to recover from. Veterans:

> ...*returned home, picked up the pieces, and moved on. But some could never find that peace. The first step was returning home. Hundreds of thousands of soldiers traveled by train, horse and foot. Southern soldiers often had the hardest time getting back to their loved ones. Upon returning home, some soldiers might have found that the life they had left behind was gone. ...If it wasn't the veteran putting himself in the asylum there are even records I have come across where a wife or family will admit their loved one and sometimes under false pretenses in order to gain access to their pension.*[79]

The change in them and the change they returned to was overwhelming to some. Only those who had grit and could bounce back and build resilience into their thought processes would move on to contribute to the rebuilding of America from the destruction.

Veteran life stories.

---

[77] va.gov; See *America's Wars - US Department of Veterans Affairs.*

[78] census.gov; See *History and Growth of the United States Census: 1790-1890.*

[79] soldierstudies.org; See *What Happened to Civil War Soldiers After the War?*

Warrior to Patriot Citizen

- **George Washington Williams** (1849–1891) American historian, clergyman, politician, lawyer, and lecturer, enlisted in the Union Army when he was only 14. He was the first person to write an objective and scientifically researched history of black people in the United States, *History of the Negro Race in America*, and later became a minister.
- **William Cody** (1846-1917) enlisted as a teamster with the rank of private in Company H, 7th Kansas Cavalry and served until discharged in 1865. Later, he scouted for Indians and fought in 16 battles and then was contracted to supply bison meat for the Army and the Kansas Pacific Railroad, thus earning his nickname of "Buffalo Bill."
- **Louisa May Alcott** (1832-1888) was a nurse during the Civil War who later became a writer, with over 30 books to her credit. *Little Women*, her most famous book, departed from the existing practice of stereotypical children in books, instead offering a fully realized young heroine in the spirited character of tomboy Jo March. One might wonder if her military experience influenced her writing style.

Veteran Legislation during the 1800s. From the Revolutionary War up to the start of the Civil War, veteran pensions were varied, focused on compensation not only to the veteran himself, but his widows and children as well. Too often, though, legislation took years to come to fruition. The veteran pension system of the U.S. began:

> *...August 26, 1776, in a resolution of the Continental Congress providing that every commissioned officer, non-commissioned officer and private soldier who shall lose a limb in any engagement, or be so disabled in the service of the United States of America as to render him incapable of afterwards getting a livelihood, shall receive during his life or the*

continuance of such disability the one-half of his monthly pay from and after the time that his pay as an officer [or soldier] ceases.[80]

The original pension legislation started the process of veteran legislation, but the legislative text became voluminous, and progress until the revision of the pension laws in 1873 was chaotic.

1818 Service Pension Law. Historian John P. Reach writes about this legislation:

> *The Revolutionary War Pension Act of 1818 created new public policy. The act provided lifetime pensions to veterans who served at least nine months in the Continental Army and who were also "in reduced circumstances" and "in need of assistance from [their] country for support."*[81]

The act broke the dam of congressional resistance against awarding lifetime pensions to veterans for their completion of military service. It created the first national military pension, which also replaced state service pensions operated by a few states.

The *Act of 14 February 1871* granted pensions to surviving soldiers and sailors who had served 60 days in the War of 1812 and had been honorably discharged, or to those who had been personally named in any resolution by Congress for specific service of less than 60 days. The widows of such soldiers and sailors were eligible for pension provided the marriage had taken place before the treaty of peace was ratified on 17 February 1815.

---

[80] socialwelfarehistory.com; See *Veteran's Pensions: Early History*, by Edward F. Waite.

[81] *Politics and Public Culture: The Revolutionary War Pension Act of 1818*, by John P. Resch.

The Act of 9 March 1878 provided pensions for surviving soldiers and sailors of the War of 1812 who had served for 14 days or in any engagement and had been honorably discharged and for their surviving widows. It made no proviso regarding the date of marriage.

The Mexican Veteran Pension Law of 1887 extended previous enacted veteran legislation of veteran pensions for "disabilities or dependencies" for widows and orphans, and was approved January 29, 1887. It stated the Secretary of the Interior be, and was thereby, authorized and directed:

> *...to place on the pension-roll the names of the surviving officers and enlisted men, including marines, militia, and volunteers, of the military and naval services of the United States, who, being duly enlisted, actually served sixty days with the Army or Navy of the United States in Mexico.*

Dependent and Disability Pension Act of 1890. The act provided pensions for all veterans who had served at least ninety days in the Union military or naval forces, were honorably discharged from service and were unable to perform manual labor, regardless of their financial situation or when the disability was suffered. Benefits were also expanded to veterans' parents, widows, and children.

1900s Wars, Conflicts, and Legislation

The advances in technology and inventiveness to warfare and its support accelerated as more people became involved during this century. The U.S. was becoming a national "teenager" among the First World nations in the first half of the 1900s, and with this national growing up came a need to handle its growth and size among the world powers.

World War I (The Great War): 1914-1918. While the U.S. supplied the Allied Powers with resources and materials, the U.S. did not enter the war in Europe until April 1917. The statistics for U.S. service members involved during World War I were: Total Service members = 4,734,991, battle deaths = 53,402, other deaths in service (non-Theater) = 63,114.[82] The domino effect of the national connections and treaties that quickly involved all of Europe within a matter of months, and later the U.S.:

> *...pitted Germany, Austria-Hungary and the Ottoman Empire (the so-called Central Powers) against Great Britain, France, Russia, Italy and Japan (the Allied Powers). The Allies were joined after 1917 by the United States. The four years of the Great War–as it was then known–saw unprecedented levels of carnage and destruction, thanks to grueling trench warfare and the introduction of modern weaponry such as machine guns, tanks and chemical weapons.[83]*

Just as the domino effect lead up to the start of the war, so did it create the fall and the ultimate surrenders of the Central Powers. The Great War ended in November 1918, 20 months after the U.S. entered it. Over nine million people had been killed and 21 million more wounded. Because of the changes in warfare, changes also occurred for veterans soon after the war began. U.S. programs for disability compensation, insurance for service personnel and veterans, and vocational rehabilitation for the disabled were created by Congress to improve veteran benefits.

But of primary concern, veterans had come to resent returning from "over there" to find:

---

[82] va.gov; See *America's Wars - US Department of Veterans Affairs*
[83] www.history.com; See *World War I History.*

civilian pay had increased by 200 to 300 percent during the war while they subsisted on low levels of military pay, which remained stagnant. The newly formed American Legion began lobbying Congress to "readjust" servicemen's pay—to compensate veterans for the wages they gave up due their service.[84]

President Harding and his successor, Calvin Coolidge, understood that sound fiscal policies motivated businesses to begin investing in the U.S. economy again. The post-war recessions of 1918-1919 and 1920-1921 concerned everyone, including veterans. By 1922 the economy began to recover, but the combination of cutting the top U.S. tax rate from 73 to 58 percent in 1922 and to 25 percent in 1925 and cutting the size, scope, and growth of the Federal government through attrition would create an economy that significantly rebounded and created the Roaring Twenties.[85]

To make up for the service members' low pay during WWI, Congress promised a bonus, but to get the measure past stringent fiscal conservatives, they delayed paying the bonus until 1945. While it took about 40 years to provide a pension to indigent veterans during the Revolutionary War and the Mexican-American War, WWI veterans were to receive it much sooner. Later, Hoover and Roosevelt (FDR) reversed the sound fiscal policies of the 1920s by raising taxes to 75 percent again.[86]

High unemployment during the Great Depression caused veterans to demand earlier bonus payments, because in some cases that was the only thing they had of value to them and their families. In 1932, Congress enacted legislation that stated each veteran received a bonus

---

[84] *Serving America's Veterans*, by Korb, Duggan, Juul, and Bergmann, p. 21.
[85] cato.org; See *1920s Income Tax Cuts Sparked Economic Growth and Raised Federal Revenues.*
[86] wikipedia.org; See *Revenue Act of 1935.*

which could not be cashed in until 1945, but in 1936 Congress overrode FDR's veto and allowed veterans to cash in their bonus nine years early.

Veteran life stories.

- **John Caspar Wister** (1887-1982), acting First Sergeant of the Advance Ordnance, Depot 4, Haute Marne, France, wrote an unusual book of memoirs from World War I. He was a serviceman who was never at the front, never heard gunfire, never saw an enemy soldier, but after the war went on to become one of the United States' most highly honored horticulturists.

- **Edwin Hubble** (1889-1953) quickly finished his Ph.D. dissertation, *Photographic Investigations of Faint Nebulae,* at the University of Chicago in 1917. He then volunteered in the U.S. Army and rose to the rank of Lt. Col. during the war, but never saw combat. Hubble is generally regarded as one of the most important observational cosmologists of the 20th century.

World War II: 1941-1945. As the veteran legislation over WWI veteran bonus money concluded in the mid-1930s, a more ominous threat was lurking on the horizon: World War II. While the war started in 1939, America did not enter it until the bombing of Pearl Harbor in December 1941. Service statistics for WWII included a total of U.S. service members (worldwide) = 16,112,566, battle deaths = 291,557, and other deaths = 113,842.[87] But the numbers of those involved and affected are much higher.

World War II became the deadliest conflict in human history. The end of the war culminated in V-E Day (Victory over Europe) and V-J Day (Victory over Japan).[88] While previous wars saw fewer numbers of veterans and legislation for veterans coming years or even decades after their wars, WWII was different. With 16 million veterans coming

---

[87] va.gov; See *America's Wars - US Department of Veterans Affairs.*
[88] wikipedia.org; See *World War II.*

home after the war, there was exhilaration and relief... and uneasiness. Politicians, the troops coming home, and everyone in between wondered, "Now what?"[89]

During WWI, returning veterans got a ticker tape parades and re-entered civilian life facing a couple of economic recessions soon after the war ended as nations began to retool and rebuild. The "bonus" bills were paid about 17 years after the war. On the other hand, the WWII wartime economy was a boom for civilians.[90]

As a national economy switches from peace to war and back again, there's an expectation that time is needed to reacquire a peacetime footing and business and economic readjustments needed switching to a peacetime economy. Veterans, again, would have the more difficult time with the readjustments. FDR's comments concerning veterans were:

> ...*the members of the armed forces have been compelled to make greater economic sacrifice and every other kind of sacrifice than the rest of us, and they are entitled to definite action to help take care of their special problems.*[91]

FDR was focused on passing veteran legislation as far back as 1940, in anticipation of exiting the war and drawing down the military forces after the war ended. He made preparations for mustering-out pay and unemployment insurance to counter the issues the doughboys of WWI experienced.[92]

Veteran life stories.

- **Jackie Robinson** (1919-1972), baseball pioneer, was drafted in 1942 and rose to the rank of second lieutenant. Robinson broke

---

[89] *Over Here: How the G.I. Bill transformed the American Dream*, by Edward Humes, p. 6.
[90] Humes, p. 14.
[91] Korb, Duggan, Juul, and Bergmann, p. 27.
[92] Korb, Duggan, Juul, and Bergmann, p. 26-28.

the baseball color barrier when the Brooklyn Dodgers started him at first base on April 15, 1947.

- **Medgar Evers** (1925-1963) was drafted into the U.S. Army in 1943, fought in both France and Germany during World War II, and received an honorable discharge in 1946. He then became a civil rights activist from Mississippi, involved in efforts to overturn segregation at the University of Mississippi.

Korean War: 1950-1953. The Korean War became the first flare-up during the Cold War. Total U.S. Service members worldwide = 5,720,000, battle deaths = 33,739, other deaths = 20,507.[93]

Veteran life stories.

- **James Earl Jones** (1931-) actor and activist, was in the Army ROTC in college and commissioned an Army officer, getting out after making 1st Lieutenant. He left the service and moved to New York, where he worked as a janitor and studied at the American Theatre Wing before becoming a very successful actor.
- **Arnold Palmer** (1929-) was well regarded as an amateur golfer at Wake Forest University, but after a personal tragedy, he entered the Coast Guard from 1951-1953. His commanding officer, Rear Adm. Roy L. Raney, recommended Palmer pursue a career as a Coast Guard officer, but Palmer decided his shot was at the PGA Tour.[94]

Viet Nam Conflict: 1960s-1970s. The Viet Nam Conflict became an extension of the Korean War, and thus the Cold War. Total U.S. Service members worldwide = 8,744,000, battle deaths = 47,434, other deaths = 42,786.[95]

---

[93] va.gov; See *America's Wars - US Department of Veterans Affairs.*
[94] coastguard.dodlive.mil; See *Arnold Palmer: Golfer & Coast Guardsman.*
[95] va.gov; See *America's Wars - US Department of Veterans Affairs.*

Veteran life stories.

- **Bob Ross** (1942-1995) entered the USAF as a medical records technician and retired in 1981 as a First Sergeant. His love of painting came after being stationed in Alaska, and he was later hired by PBS in 1982 to host his *The Joy of Painting* show. His post retirement income came not from his show, which he did for free, but from Bob Ross the corporation, with 20 how-to books, 100 videotapes, a line of Bob Ross art materials, and 150 art teachers teaching his methods.[96]

- **Kris Kristofferson** (1936-) obtained a BA in literature from Pomona College in 1958, and later earned a scholarship to Oxford. He joined the Army under parental pressure and became a helicopter pilot after completing Ranger school, working his way up to the rank of Captain. He was offered a teaching position in Literature at West Point, but he turned it down to focus on music. He later became a highly regarded singer/songwriter and actor.[97]

Persian Gulf War I: 1990-1991. Iraqi leader Saddam Hussein ordered the invasion and occupation of neighboring Kuwait in early August 1990. Fellow Arab powers such as Saudi Arabia and Egypt called on the United States and other Western nations to intervene.

In response, a coalition of 34 nations waged a war codenamed *Operation Desert Shield* (August 2, 1990-January 17, 1991) for operations leading to the buildup of troops and defense of Saudi Arabia, and *Operation Desert Storm* (January 17, 1991-February 28, 1991) in its combat phase. The Coalition defeated the Iraqis 100 hours after the ground campaign started. Total U.S. Service members = 2,322,000, battle deaths = 148, other deaths = 1,800.[98]

---

[96] articles.orlandosentinel.com; See *Bob Ross Uses His Brush to Spread Paint and Joy.*
[97] military.com; See *Famous Veteran: Kris Kristofferson.*
[98] va.gov; See *America's Wars - US Department of Veterans Affairs.*

Veteran life stories.
- **Richard Burrell** (1968-) was a field artillery cannon crewman with a firing battery from the 10th Marine Regiment during the first Gulf War. Since the war, he's become a full-time musician.

Legislation during the 1900s. No fewer than 75 bills were introduced in Congress soon after the Great War ended to provide a "bonus" to veterans. But Presidents Wilson through to FDR and Congress worked at maneuvering some form of "bonus," or certificate, compensation through the budgetary minefield with the ever-moving political target of taxes and spending and responsibilities toward veterans. Included in this political chaos, the Veterans Bureau came under scrutiny when less than 25% of veteran disability claims were processed even though over 200,000 people were wounded in the early 1920s.[99] Following WWI, Congress established the Veterans Administration, which consolidated three different federal agencies: The Veterans Bureau, the Bureau of Pensions, and the National Home for Disabled Volunteer Soldiers. Later, the GI Bill became the gold standard that all other veteran legislation is measured against.

War Risk Insurance Act Amendments of 1917 provided government-subsidized life insurance. Amendments added provisions for rehab and vocational training for permanently disabled veterans.

Vocation Rehabilitation Act of 1918 gives allowances to veterans unable to work and extra benefits to the honorably discharged who are disabled.

World War Adjustment Compensation Act of 1924 provided bonuses to veterans based on length of service, but they would not be paid until 1945. Many veterans applied, but were denied benefits and never reapplied. Because of the change from a war economy to a business economy, changes in the marketplace caused changes in the economy,

---

[99] Korb, Duggan, Juul, and Bergmann, pp. 20-21.

and many veterans, disabled or not, could not find work. Indeed, some cities passed ordinances that required veterans with severe facial wounds to wear masks or hoods in order not to scare women and children. About 8,0000-10,000 veterans with "shell shock" found it difficult to get hired, as employers didn't want mental breakdowns while they were on the job. Public sympathy waned over time, and government efforts were ineffective at treating veterans.[100]

While the veteran political process ground on, sound bites carried through at every point. President Coolidge cited fiscal concerns for vetoing any bills, and added, "Patriotism which is bought and paid for is not patriotism." Representative Cochran, a Missouri Democrat, said the bonus "is not a dole, a handout, it is an adjustment in a very small degree of the soldier's pay while he served his country."[101]

Servicemen's Readjustment Act of 1944 was the beginnings of the G.I. Bill, and provided unemployment compensation, home and farm loans, and educational benefits. This bill was even more liberalized in 1945; and when veteran eligibility ended in the mid-1950s, about 51 percent, or 7.8 million veterans, took advantage of the educational benefits, with one-third going to college and the rest attending vocational or other education.

Veterans' Preference Act of 1944 required the federal government to favor returning war veterans when hiring new employees in an attempt to recognize their service, sacrifice, and skills.

The *Veterans' Readjustment Assistance Act of 1952,* also called the Korean GI Bill, extended the benefits of the GI Bill to Korean War veterans.

The *Veterans' Readjustment Benefits Act of 1966* followed World War II and the Korean War legislation, but little by little, veterans realized that the benefits weren't nearly as comprehensive as previous GI Bills.

---

[100] *Issues of Returning Soldiers from WW1;* presentation by Jocelyn Martin, Feb 2014.
[101] Korb, Duggan, Juul, and Bergmann, pp. 22-23.

In addition, only 10 percent of available hospital beds were occupied by Vietnam veterans, and complaints found the VA unresponsive to the needs of those veterans.

The *Vietnam Veterans' Psychological Readjustment Act of 1979* marked the first major legislation victory for Vietnam veterans. In 1978, the American Psychiatric Association recognized post-traumatic stress disorder (PTSD), a significant problem among Vietnam vets.[102] The act offered 232 community-based readjustment counseling centers staffed by three or four "paraprofessionals" to help veterans.

In 1989, Congress passed legislation that transformed the Veterans Administration into the Department of Veterans Affairs, and elevated the Secretary of Veterans Affairs (formerly the "Administrator") to a Cabinet level position. The DVA is responsible for almost all federal programs that provide benefits to military veterans.

2000s Wars, Conflicts, and Legislation

Afghanistan/Iraq/WoT/GWOT Wars: 2001 - Present. The War on Terror (WoT), also known as the Global War on Terrorism (GWOT), refers to the international military campaign that started after the September 11, 2001 attacks on the United States. The Afghanistan war started soon afterward, while the Second Iraq War (Gulf War II) started in March 2003. This war may not be over any time soon, and more chapters are being added to its story every year.

Veteran life stories. Veteran stories have been and are being written as we speak. Included are the "living stories" of veterans who are among us now who can tell what they went through. These stories, which need to be told, should be written by our veterans themselves for a number of reasons. First, when veterans write about their

---

[102] *Ibid*, pp. 32-33.

experiences (including expressive writing or writing therapy[103]), it preserves a small part of military history and for those that need it, is cathartic. Second, there's an old saying that states, "When an old person dies, a library burns to the ground." When veterans write their stories, it provides a connection between the older generation that has served with the younger generations who want to serve and want to learn the wisdom from those that went before them. This also applies to learning about their various jobs, careers, and experiences. Lastly and most importantly, it preserves a part of a veteran's life for their families to reflect on as life marches on.

Legislation during the 2000s. Thousands of veterans who have served in Afghanistan, Iraq, and the GWOT need acknowledgement and support from the rest of America. As a veteran, you need to tell your story to the rest of America so others can grasp the help needed by you and our brothers and sisters who have served. The mantra is, "If we send them, we must mend them" approach.

You will find more individual veteran stories at *Experiencing War: Stories from the Veteran History Project* at the Library of Congress web site (loc.org).

---

[103] vietnow.com; See *PTSD: Writing - A pathway for healing trauma.*

The two most important days in your life are the day you are born, and the day you find out why. —Samuel Langhorne Clemens